THE BEDFORD SERIES IN HISTORY AND CULTURE

The French Revolution and Human Rights

A Brief History with Documents

SECOND EDITION

Lynn Hunt

University of California, Los Angeles

bedford/st.martin's
Macmillan Learning
Boston | New York

For Bedford/St. Martin's

Vice President, Editorial, Macmillan Learning Humanities: Edwin Hill
Publisher for History: Michael Rosenberg
Acquiring Editor for History: Laura Arcari
Director of Development for History: Jane Knetzger
Developmental Editor: Melanie McFadyen
Executive Marketing Manager: Sandra McGuire
Production Editor: Lidia MacDonald-Carr
Production Coordinator: Carolyn Quimby
Director of Rights and Permissions: Hilary Newman
Permissions Assistant: Michael McCarty
Permissions Manager: Kalina Ingham
Cover Design: William Boardman
Cover Photo: France, Paris. *Declaration of the Rights of Man and of the Citizen* / Musée
de la Ville de Paris, Musée Carnavalet, Paris, France / De Agostini Picture Library /
G. Dagli Orti / Bridgeman Images
Project Management: Books By Design, Inc.
Composition: Achorn International, Inc.
Printing and Binding: RR Donnelley and Sons

Manufactured in the United States of America.

0   9   8
f   e   d   c   b

For information, write: Bedford/St. Martin's, 75 Arlington Street, Boston, MA 02116
(617-399-4000)

ISBN 978-1-319-04903-4

Acknowledgments

*Acknowledgments and copyrights appear on the same pages as the text and art selections
they cover; these acknowledgments and copyrights constitute an extension of the copyright
page. It is a violation of the law to reproduce these selections by any means whatsoever
without the written permission of the copyright holder.*

Foreword

The Bedford Series in History and Culture is designed so that readers can study the past as historians do. The historian's first task is finding the evidence. Documents, letters, memoirs, interviews, pictures, movies, novels, or poems can provide facts and clues. Then the historian questions and compares the sources. There is more to do than in a courtroom, for hearsay evidence is welcome, and the historian is usually looking for answers beyond act and motive. Different views of an event may be as important as a single verdict. How a story is told may yield as much information as what it says.

Along the way the historian seeks help from other historians and perhaps from specialists in other disciplines. Finally, it is time to write, to decide on an interpretation and how to arrange the evidence for readers.

Each book in this series contains an important historical document or group of documents, each document a witness from the past and open to interpretation in different ways. The documents are combined with some element of historical narrative—an introduction or a biographical essay, for example—that provides students with an analysis of the primary source material and important background information about the world in which it was produced.

Each book in the series focuses on a specific topic within a specific historical period. Each provides a basis for lively thought and discussion about several aspects of the topic and the historian's role. Each is short enough (and inexpensive enough) to be a reasonable one-week assignment in a college course. Whether as classroom or personal reading, each book in the series provides firsthand experience of the challenge—and fun—of discovering, recreating, and interpreting the past.

Lynn Hunt
David W. Blight
Bonnie G. Smith

Preface

The language of human rights frames much of the world's discussion about politics. Complaints about repressive or undemocratic regimes often focus on their "human rights record," and in the United States and other Western countries internal political discussions often center on rights questions, from the conflicts over abortion rights to campaigns for the rights of women, minorities, gays, lesbians, and transgender people, the disabled, and people with AIDS. Although many people take the existence of rights for granted, there is much less certainty about where rights come from, how they are justified, or which ones really count. One way to grasp the concept of rights is to look at one of the most extensive and concentrated discussions of them: during the French Revolution, particularly between 1789 and 1794.

As in the first edition of this book, the introduction (Part One) shows how the discussion of rights during the French Revolution built upon the seventeenth- and eighteenth-century origins of the idea of human rights (then expressed as the "rights of man"). It also provides an overview of the consequences of putting rights into practice once the Revolution began: the rights of Protestants and Jews in that largely Catholic country, the rights of free blacks and slaves, the rights of the poor and those without property, the rights of women, and even the rights of actors and executioners, who had been excluded from many rights in the past. The French revolutionaries also confronted the need to reconcile and, at times, sacrifice individual rights to their version of national security. Their discussions anticipated many of the debates that shaped politics and social life in the nineteenth and twentieth centuries, and thus provide an excellent introduction to the issues of modern civic life.

The documents in Part Two are divided into four main categories that convey the breadth and depth of the questions raised about rights. Chapter 1, "Defining Rights before 1789," shows that religious toleration, opposition to slavery, and concerns about the rights of women had begun to draw attention even before 1789. Chapter 2, "The Declaration

of the Rights of Man and Citizen, 1789," delves into the debates surrounding the Declaration; despite the contested nature of the Declaration, it would go on to exert great influence in human rights thinking for
two centuries and therefore bears close scrutiny. Chapter 3, "Debates
over Citizenship and Rights during the Revolution," covers the contro-
versies that ensued over the rights of those without property, religious
minorities, free blacks and slaves, and women.

Chapter 4, "National Security and Limits on Rights," is new to this
second edition. While the French revolutionaries extended individual
rights further than ever before imagined in Europe or the Americas, they
also developed new forms of suppression of rights that they justified in
the name of saving the nation. The French revolutionaries first developed their notion of the "nation" as a counterweight to the king, arguing that even in a constitutional monarchy sovereignty should rest first
and foremost in the nation itself. Over time they came to see the nation
as superior to any intermediate interest such as trade associations or
religious organizations, and as dissent grew and war created a sense of
national emergency, individual rights were increasingly infringed. The
documents in this new chapter aim to give readers a sense of the issues
involved.

Several editorial features have been designed to help the reader understand the historical context of the documents and the questions about
human rights that they raise. They include document headnotes, a chro-
nology, questions for consideration, a selected bibliography, and an index.
I have translated all the documents except where noted, and I am solely
responsible for any mistakes or infelicities that remain.

ACKNOWLEDGMENTS

Many people helped me during the preparation of this collection of
documents: Elizabeth Colwill, Denise Davidson, Suzanne Desan, Aaron
Freeman, Paul Hanson, Jeff Horn, Gary Kates, and Bryant Ragan Jr. Jeremy Popkin suggested that I include more on the suppression of rights
for this new edition. A National Endowment for the Humanities fellow-
ship provided funding at the most critical time. At Bedford/St. Martin's,
I thank Publisher Michael Rosenberg, Acquiring Editor Laura Arcari,
Director of Development Jane Knetzger, Executive Marketing Manager
Sandra McGuire, Developmental Editor Melanie McFadyen, Production

Editor Lidia MacDonald-Carr, Cover Designer William Boardman, and Production Coordinator Nancy Benjamin of Books By Design. I am sure that I have learned as much from my students (including others not here named) over the years as they have learned from me, so it is only fitting that I dedicate this book to them.

Lynn Hunt

Contents

Illustrations

PART ONE

Introduction:
The Revolutionary Origins
of Human Rights

"Human rights" is perhaps the most discussed and least understood of political terms in the early twenty-first century. Even its precise definition is uncertain: Does it include the right to a "living wage," for example, or the right to a protected ethnic identity? In the eighteenth century, many writers distinguished between *political* and *civil* rights: Political rights guaranteed equal participation in voting, officeholding, and other aspects of political participation; civil rights guaranteed equal treatment before the law in matters concerning marriage, property, and inheritance, that is, nonpolitical matters. In recent decades the distinction between political and civil rights has been blurred because, increasingly, people assume that individuals should enjoy both (hence the more general term *human rights*), and other rights have been progressively added to the list: the right to nondiscrimination in employment or housing, the right to a basic level of welfare, and the like.

Despite—or perhaps because of—its vagueness, the concept of human rights commands widespread public support, especially in the Western world but also worldwide. In 1948, the United Nations made human rights the standard of international justice by adopting a Universal Declaration of Human Rights. It proclaimed that "recognition of the inherent dignity and of the equal and inalienable rights of all members of the human family is the foundation of freedom, justice and peace in the world."[1]

1

This broad claim summarizes the essence of the concept of human rights as it has developed since the seventeenth century. To declare the existence and political relevance of human rights in this fashion implies that (1) all human beings have certain inherent rights simply by virtue of being human, and not by virtue of their status in society; (2) these rights are consequently imagined as "natural," as stemming from human nature itself, and they have in the past often been called "natural rights"; (3) rights belong therefore to individuals and not to any social group, whether a sex, a race, an ethnicity, a group of families, a social class, an occupational group, a nation, or the like; (4) these rights must be made equally available by law to all individuals and cannot be denied as long as an individual lives under the law; (5) the legitimacy of any government rests on its ability to guarantee the rights of all its members.

These conditions might seem straightforward to us now, but they imply a break with all the traditional ideas of government dominant in the world before the end of the eighteenth century and continuing in influence in many places even today. Traditionally, rulers exercised supreme power because something about their persons (royal birth, military success, or religious leadership) made them closer to God than ordinary mortals, and whole groups within society (such as nobles) enjoyed certain privileges depending on the customs and traditions of the country. Privileges depended on social rank in a vertical hierarchy distinguishing higher from lower groups, whereas human rights rest on an implicitly horizontal conception of society in which all politically active individuals possess the same rights by their nature as humans.

Several contrasts follow from the fundamental differences in the way society is conceived. People who believe in human rights emphasize the sanctity of the individual, imagined to be like all other individuals; traditional governments stressed the sanctity of one individual, the king or queen, and the importance of social differences. The notion of human rights tends to favor democracy; traditional ideas of social difference supported aristocracy and monarchy. Religion could and did justify both conceptions; but in the long run the believers in human rights often insisted on a separation between church and state, whereas upholders of traditional ideas argued for a close connection between religion and politics. Thus human rights was an idea with great consequences; more than any other notion, it has defined the nature of modern politics and society.

In theory, according to the UN declaration of 1948, all people are equally entitled to human rights. Article 1 of the declaration asserted that "All human beings are born free and equal in dignity and rights." The application of the theory is far from perfect, of course, even at the beginning of the twenty-first century. And the theory itself has been questioned in some quarters. Ever since the concept of human rights emerged in the late seventeenth and eighteenth centuries, there has buun persistent debate about its value and pertinence. In the early nineteenth century, for example, the English political philosopher and social reformer Jeremy Bentham insisted that "Natural rights is simple nonsense; natural and imprescriptible rights (an American phrase), rhetorical nonsense, nonsense upon stilts."[2] Later in the nineteenth century some argued that rights belonged only to communities or nations, not individuals. More recently, some nations have rejected the relevance of human rights to their lands, arguing that human rights is only a Western notion and hence unsuited to other cultures.

But even when and where the idea of rights gained acceptance—as in the British North American colonies of the eighteenth century—the meaning of those rights became a subject of intense debate (and, in the United States, ultimately the subject of a civil war in the 1860s). In many ways the political history of the Western world since the early eighteenth century has been dominated by the issue of rights: Do they exist, what are they, who enjoys them, and what means are justified in protecting and establishing them? The concept of rights has constantly expanded since its first articulations: From its origins in discussion about the rights of propertied men and religious minorities, it has slowly but almost inevitably grown to include women, nonwhites, and every other kind of minority from homosexuals to the disabled.

Most debates about rights originated in the eighteenth century, and nowhere were discussions of them more explicit, more divisive, or more influential than in revolutionary France in the 1790s. The answers given then to the most fundamental questions about rights have remained relevant ever since. The framers of the UN declaration of 1948 closely followed the model established by the French Declaration of the Rights of Man and Citizen of 1789, while substituting "human" for the more ambiguous "man" throughout. Article 1 of the French declaration of 1789 decreed, for instance, that "Men are born and remain free and equal in rights," virtually the identical language of the first article of the 1948 declaration.

DEFINING RIGHTS BEFORE 1789

The idea of universal human rights *is* Western in origin. It did not appear all at once but slowly emerged in the eighteenth century, in large part as a reaction to contemporary political conflicts—in Great Britain, between Great Britain and its North American colonies, and in France.

Its sources varied from new conceptions of individual autonomy (the belief that individuals should make their own decisions about marriage, for example) to debates about the foundations of government.[3] What is most distinctive about Western notions of human rights is the emphasis on their universal applicability; by implication, human rights are for all humans, not just for one nation or group.

This universalism has many roots, ranging from the Western notion of "natural law," which had precedents going back all the way to the Greeks, to the less exalted influence of Western imperialism and colonialism, which encouraged the conviction that Europeans could determine what was best for other peoples too. Philosophers, such as Hugo Grotius in 1625, argued that natural laws derived from the study of human nature, not religion; that they did not vary by historical context; and that they therefore existed independently of all political powers and authorities. In other words, natural law stood above the current historical and political context and served as a measuring rod against which any actual laws or governments could be judged. Ironically, ideas of natural law and especially natural rights were soon picked up by the opponents of Western imperialism and colonialism and used to attack the subjugation of other peoples; colonizing them, they argued, destroyed their natural rights.

The social contract theory put forth by John Locke in 1690 provided a crucial link between natural law and universal rights; he held that all government rested on an implicit social contract rooted in human nature. The social contract expressed natural laws and served to protect natural rights. But what were those rights and was everyone equally entitled to them? In one of the most enduringly influential formulations of human rights, Locke maintained that all *men* had a natural right to life, liberty, and property:

> Man being born, as has been proved, with a Title to perfect Freedom, and an uncontrolled enjoyment of all the Rights and Privileges of the Law of Nature, equally with any other Man, or Number of Men in the World, hath by Nature a Power, not only to preserve his Property, that is, his Life, Liberty and Estate, against the Injuries and Attempts of other Men; but to judge of, and punish the breaches of that Law in others.[4]

In Locke's view government should be designed to protect these rights. If it did not, then it could be justifiably overthrown, as the English Parliament had overthrown King Charles I in the 1640s. Just what Locke meant, however, by "man" or "men" has long been the subject of debate.

When Locke wrote at the end of the seventeenth century, he had in mind the rights of European (and particularly English) male property owners, not poor propertyless men, not women, not slaves. Locke himself invested money in the English slave trade and justified slavery as the legal fruit of wars of conquest.

The French philosophers and propagandists of the eighteenth-century intellectual movement known as the Enlightenment wanted to go further than Locke in their definition of natural rights, although they disagreed about just how far. Like Locke, Jean-Jacques Rousseau insisted in 1762 that society and government could be based not on tradition, custom, habit, or history but only on rational principles. But unlike Locke, Rousseau believed that these principles should apply to all men, whether kings or peasants, property owners or propertyless, French or Tahitians. In other words, Rousseau's vision was even more universalistic than Locke's. Yet Rousseau, like other Enlightenment thinkers, never precisely defined rights beyond the right of all men to participate in making the social contract. Enlightenment writers held that reason revealed self-evident truths and that among those truths were the natural rights of all peoples; for some at least this meant slaves as well as property owners, although few—and certainly not Rousseau—thought it included women as well as men.

The article "Natural Law" from the French *Encyclopedia* (1755)—see Document 1—summarized many of these eighteenth-century Enlightenment views. Unlike present-day encyclopedias, the French one edited by Denis Diderot and Jean d' Alembert between 1751 and 1780 provoked immediate political and religious controversy. It challenged many beliefs and customs of its time and earned its editors constant government harassment and condemnation by the Catholic Church. The article on natural law might seem at first glance to be tamely abstract. It argued that natural law was a familiar idea because it was based on reason and common human feeling. It went on to insist that by natural law the "general will" provides the only foundation of social and political duties. The general will, in turn, teaches people how to determine their natural rights. Thus this general will based on reason and nature had very little in common with the usual justifications of monarchy; indeed, the concept of general will, often defined as the will of all, might conceivably legitimize democracy instead (as it did in the writings of Rousseau, another contributor to the *Encyclopedia*).

Like most other monarchies in the eighteenth century—and monarchy was the dominant form of government everywhere in the world at the time—the French monarchy based its legitimacy on "divine right":

Monarchs ruled because God had chosen them for their positions. Kings (queens, being women, were more problematic and in France could never rule in their own names) were imagined as literally closer to God than were other humans. Kings occupied the highest positions among humans on the great chain that stretched from God down through humans to all the lowliest creatures on earth; they consequently had a religious aura about them. Aristocrats, because of their noble birth, were higher than commoners; merchants were higher than servants; and so on. An individual's position was determined by his or her rank, literally one's place in a vertical hierarchy (a woman's rank was determined by her father's before marriage and by her husband's after marriage). One's privileges followed from this social position.

The *Encyclopedia*, in contrast, spoke the language of equal, individual human rights: "I am a man, and I have no other true, inalienable *natural rights* than those of humanity." The article on natural law, written by Diderot himself, made no mention of social differences or, for that matter, of kings. Indeed, it concluded with a clear challenge to the monarchy: "the laws should be made for everyone, and not for one person [presumably the king]." Like other mid-eighteenth-century Enlightenment thinkers, Diderot never specified the content of those "true, inalienable *natural rights*" of humanity. His article advocated the use of reason to determine them yet stopped short of actually providing a list. This reticence probably made sense, given the situation: The mere insistence on "natural" rights might be viewed as threatening to established authorities. Moreover, because the French monarchy considered itself above ordinary mortals and closely tied to the Catholic religion, it tolerated neither open criticism of its policies nor variations in religious practice. Even such vague formulations as that of the *Encyclopedia*'s on natural law brought down the wrath of French censors.

The idea of human rights nonetheless steadily gained ground in the eighteenth century, propelled by the campaigns for religious toleration and the abolition of slavery. In 1685, Louis XIV had revoked all the rights and privileges of French Calvinists (Protestants who followed the teachings of the French-born reformer Jean Calvin), requiring them to convert to Catholicism. The king ordered the destruction of all their churches, forbade any public form of their worship, confiscated the property of any Calvinist who fled, and condemned to the galleys any pastor who refused to renounce his religion. One hundred fifty thousand Calvinists immediately fled into exile, but many others stayed behind to practice their religion secretly. Despite widespread support for this policy within the country, criticism both inside and outside of France grew steadily, and it did much to fuel the Enlightenment as a movement for reform.

Over the course of the eighteenth century, public opinion gradually became more favorable to the Calvinists (the Crown did not persecute the Lutherans in the newly conquered eastern provinces because there were no Lutherans in the rest of France).[5] The Calas Affair brought reform sentiment to a boil. In 1761 the son of the Calvinist Jean Calas apparently committed suicide by hanging himself at home. The family did not report it as such because suicide was considered a crime and entailed a humiliating public trial of the cadaver. Believing rumors that Calas had killed his son to prevent his conversion from Calvinism to Catholicism, local magistrates condemned the father to torture and death. In a punishment all too typical of eighteenth-century penal methods, the executioner first broke Calas's bones with an iron rod and then completed the destruction by pulling his limbs apart on a wheel. Throughout these torments, Calas refused to confess, insisting on his innocence to the end. After the execution, the Enlightenment writer Voltaire took up the family's cause and eventually won official rehabilitation of Calas's reputation and compensation for the family. During the controversy, Voltaire wrote his *Treatise on Toleration* (1763) — see Document 2 — in which he argued that freedom of conscience was guaranteed by natural law and that religious toleration would help ensure social stability and prosperity. The French government immediately seized copies of the book and imprisoned people caught distributing it.

After decades of mounting criticism and the conversion of leading officials to the cause of reform, the French monarchy finally gave way and granted, with much reluctance, certain civil rights to Calvinists. The Edict of Toleration of 1787 (see Document 3) used the new language of rights, but in a very restricted fashion. Rights, in the government's usage, were not universal or inherent but, rather, limited privileges bestowed by monarchical favor. In fact, the Latin roots of the word *privilege* translate as "private law" (*privus* = private, *legem* = law), the very antithesis of rights based on universal, natural law. The edict offered the rights of civil status (legally recognized births, marriages, and deaths), property and inheritance, and freedom to choose a profession, but it refused all political rights to Calvinists, including the right to hold judicial or municipal offices. Not surprisingly, many felt less than satisfied by these concessions. One Calvinist leader, Rabaut Saint Etienne, wrote to the government with pointed criticisms (see Document 4). Most strikingly, he complained about the government's use of the phrase "natural rights," arguing that anyone who truly believed in them would find the edict woefully inadequate.

The French government did not persecute its Jewish population as flagrantly as it did the Calvinists, but popular prejudices against them ran even more deeply. In 1686 the French monarchy decreed that Portuguese and Spanish Jews could remain in the kingdom without converting. As France acquired more territories in the east (Alsace and Lorraine) in the eighteenth century, it also absorbed a much larger Jewish population. Unlike the Portuguese and Spanish Jews who lived in southern France with manners and customs similar to other French people, the eastern Jews knew little French and were isolated even from their German-speaking neighbors because they spoke the Yiddish language and often wrote in Hebrew. By law, Jews in the eastern provinces could not live in most of the big cities or practice most occupations; they were restricted to trading in animals and secondhand clothes and to offering loans with interest, provoking in turn great animosity in the peasant-debtor population. The legal situation of the Jewish population varied from region to region and even from town to town; they had no civil rights under French law, but, unlike Calvinists, they could live in their own communities, practice their religion, and decide their political and judicial affairs for themselves, even while paying taxes to the French state.[6]

Most Enlightenment thinkers remained indifferent to the plight of the Jews in France because they did not suffer official persecution. Many, notably Voltaire, even shared popular prejudices against the Jews, considering them a separate nation with peculiar religious and cultural practices. On the one hand, Voltaire opposed persecution of the Jews, arguing, for example, "What was the Jews' crime? None other than being born." On the other hand, he often railed against Jewish customs in stereotypical fashion: "they were therefore rightly treated as a people opposed to all others, whom they served, out of greed and hatred, out of fanaticism; they made usury [the collection of exorbitant interest on loans] into a sacred duty."[7] Nonetheless, by the 1780s, partly in reaction to the discussion of the rights of Calvinists, enlightened opinion had begun to consider some kind of reform of the Jews' situation necessary. The chief literary and scientific society of Metz, a major city in eastern France, held an essay contest in 1787 and 1788 on the question "Are there means for making the Jews happier and more useful in France?"

Almost all of the contest respondents urged improvement in the status of Jews, even though they often described Jews in negative terms. One prize-winner, Abbé Grégoire, a noted advocate of human rights reform, referred to the Jews as "parasitic plants who eat away the substance of the tree to which they are attached."[8] He favored reform so that the Jews could assimilate with — become more like — the French. Even the one Jewish respondent (see Document 5) argued that reform would help make Jewish merchants more honest in their dealings.[9] Despite the depth of anti-Semitic prejudice, however, the essay contest showed that the legal status of even non-Christian minorities had now come into question. Raising the issues of utility and happiness inevitably led to discussions of rights; if the Jews were to become more useful and happier, then they would have to enjoy rights similar to those of other French people. The monarchy set up a commission to study the status of the Jews in 1788, but it never reached any decision.

Like the prejudices against the Jews, slavery had a long history in Europe, but it took a precise legal form in France only at the end of the seventeenth century, when French traders and colonists became active in the Caribbean. In the eighteenth century, both slave trading and colonial commerce in the Caribbean expanded dramatically, linked together by the establishment of sugar, indigo, coffee, and cotton plantations worked by slaves imported from Africa. At the end of the seventeenth century the French slave trade supplied the Caribbean colonies with less than one thousand slaves annually; by 1788 the annual average had risen to over thirty thousand slaves. By then, one-eighth of the French population depended on colonial commerce for their livelihoods. Like the persecution of the Calvinists, although even more slowly and hesitantly, the trading in slaves and slave-produced goods eventually aroused opposition. In Great Britain and the British North American colonies, antislavery agitation had religious roots in evangelical Protestantism, especially among the Quakers. But in mostly Catholic France, antislavery opinion originally derived from the Enlightenment's very secular emphasis on universal human rights.

The first important salvo of the French antislavery campaign was Abbé Raynal's monumental history of European colonization, *Philosophical and Political History of the Settlements and Trade of the Europeans in the East and West Indies* (see Document 6), published in 1770 but expanded and reedited many times thereafter. That this hugely detailed, multivolume history could serve as a rallying cry for reformers in both Europe and America is hard to imagine now, but it did, and spectacularly so. Raynal and his collaborators denounced all the arguments based on custom or history used to support slavery and even predicted a general slave revolt in the colonies (which in fact did take place during the French Revolution). Himself a Catholic clergyman, Raynal reserved his harshest blame for clerics who tolerated the horrors of slavery. Following the spirit of the increasingly influential natural rights tradition, Raynal relied entirely on "these eternal and immutable truths" to make his argument.

Some of the greatest beneficiaries of the social system of the French monarchy took the lead in the antislavery movement that emerged in the 1780s. In 1781 a nobleman, the Marquis de Condorcet, published a ringing condemnation of slavery (see Document 7) under the pseudonym Mister Schwartz (*schwarz* is German for "black"). He did not stop at denouncing slavery as wrong; he called it a crime because it deprived slaves of their rights. Since slavery was a crime, the masters themselves enjoyed no rights over their slaves, he concluded. Condorcet linked the fight against slavery to long-standing Enlightenment campaigns for the abolition of legal torture, reform of the criminal law codes, and restoration to the Calvinists of their civil and political rights. In the same spirit he also opposed the burning of "sodomites," the label for male homosexuals in the eighteenth century. "Sodomy," he argued, "when violence is not involved, cannot be considered a criminal offense. It violates the right of no other man."[10] Condorcet believed that so long as an activity did not violate any human rights, it should not be criminalized; likewise, whatever violated a person's rights ought to be considered a crime.

Condorcet joined the Society of the Friends of Blacks, founded in 1788 by Jacques Brissot to agitate collectively against the slave trade and slavery itself. Brissot modeled the society on the London Committee for the Abolition of the Slave Trade, established in 1787. He hoped that the groups might cooperate in an international effort to eliminate the slave trade.[11] The French society explicitly endorsed the idea of human rights; for them the first of all truths was "all men are born free." But in the still constrained atmosphere of the monarchy, they advanced their ideas (see Document 8) only in the most tentative terms, knowing that the colonial and commercial interests invested in slavery still exercised great power. As a consequence, their pamphlets argued that slavery should in principle be abolished but advocated no specific plan to achieve this end.

The most deeply rooted prejudice of all proved to be the view that women were unsuited to political life by their very nature. Although many thinkers, both male and female, had raised the question of women's status through the centuries, most of them had insisted primarily on women's right to an education (rather than on the right to vote, for instance, which few men enjoyed).[12] The status of women did not excite the same interest—as measured in terms of publications—as that of slaves, Calvinists, or even Jews in France; the issue of women's rights did not lead to essay contests, official commissions, or Enlightenment-inspired clubs under the monarchy. In part this lack of interest followed from the fact that women were not considered a persecuted group in the same way as slaves, Calvinists, or Jews. Although women's property rights and financial independence often met restrictions under French law and custom, most men and women agreed with Rousseau and other Enlightenment thinkers that women belonged in the private sphere of the home and therefore had no role to play in public affairs. Most of France's female population worked as peasants, shopkeepers, laundresses, and the like, yet women were defined primarily by their sex (and relationship in marriage) and not by their own occupations. It was consequently by no means certain that the "rights of man" were imagined as applying in the same way to women.

The woman question thus trailed behind in the wake of human rights agitation in the eighteenth century. But like all the other questions of rights, it would receive an enormous boost during the Revolution. When the monarchy faced one of its perennial financial crises in the 1780s, this one brought on by its borrowing to support the North American colonists in their war against Great Britain, its fumbling for a solution to its problems created an unprecedented situation. Failing to get agreement from the high courts (parlements) or two assemblies of notables to his proposed fiscal reforms and facing imminent bankruptcy, Louis XVI agreed to convoke a meeting of the Estates General for May 1789. The Estates General had not met since 1614, and its convocation heightened everyone's expectations for reform. The king invited the three estates— the clergy, the nobility, and the Third Estate (made up of everyone who was not a noble or a cleric) — to elect deputies through an elaborate, multilayered electoral process and to draw up lists of their grievances. At every stage of the electoral process, participants (mostly men but with a few females here and there at the parish-level meetings)[13] devoted considerable time and political negotiation to the composition of these lists of grievances. Since the king had not invited women to meet as women to draft their grievances or name delegates, a few took matters into their own hands and sent him their own petitions outlining their concerns (see Document 9). The modesty of most of these complaints and demands demonstrates the depth of the prejudice against women's separate political activity. Women could ask for better education and protection of their property rights, but even the most politically vociferous among them did not yet demand full civil and political rights.

The thousands of meetings held to elect deputies to the Estates General immediately heated up the political atmosphere. When the Estates General had last met in 1614, France had no daily newspapers and no regular postal system, making developments hard to follow. By 1789 the communications system had evolved and literacy had more than doubled (reaching 50 percent for men and 27 percent for women); mail still took a week or ten days to reach the peripheries of the country, and the government still officially controlled book and newspaper publication, but it could not hold back the flood of pamphlets that now streamed forth on every imaginable political topic.

The most pressing issue was how the Estates General would conduct its voting. The king granted the Third Estate twice the number of deputies as either the clergy of the First Estate or the nobility of the Second Estate. But he left it to the Estates General to decide whether it would vote by "order" (estate) or "head" (individually). Vote by order—each estate casting one collective vote—would give the clergy and the nobility a virtual veto over the proceedings. Vote by head would give the Third Estate the upper hand; it would need only one deputy from either of the other two orders to command a majority. The stakes were high, for the entire political future of the country depended on this decision.

A remarkably hard-hitting pamphlet (see Document 10) by a clergyman, Abbé Sieyès, crystallized much of the discussion and showed its wider implications for the nature of French society. Sieyès attacked in simple and straightforward terms every form of legal privilege and in particular assailed the nobility as a parasite—quite literally a foreign body—that sapped society. He held out a new vision of the nation in which individuals would be judged and ranked only by their contribution to productive life, not by their family background and their inherited privileges; in this nation the Third Estate would be dominant, rather than dominated by the other two estates. His pamphlet electrified readers and contributed to the Third Estate's determination to hold firm against the two "privileged" orders. Sieyès himself was elected as a deputy to the Third Estate. Even before the Revolution officially began, then, the unsettling consequences of the new notions of the individual had become apparent. "Privileges" would no longer go unchallenged; rights had to be equal in the new nation. The very idea of nobility or aristocracy was itself called into question.

THE DECLARATION OF THE RIGHTS OF MAN AND CITIZEN, 1789

The American War of Independence had helped make notions of human rights even more influential in France, for many of the French officers who served in North America arrived home fired by the ideals of liberty that they saw in action in the New World. Thomas Jefferson's Declaration of Independence of 1776 put the Enlightenment position on rights into a declarative, political form: "We hold these truths to be self-evident: that all men are created equal; that they are endowed by their Creator with certain inalienable rights; that among these are life, liberty and the pursuit of happiness" — happiness being an Enlightenment addition to Locke's original list of rights. The protection of these rights justified colonial resistance to Great Britain, but this was as far as the declaration went; it had no legal relationship to the constitutions written later.

When declaring their rights the Americans drew on the constitutional tradition that they had inherited from the English. English Parliaments regularly cited King John's Great Charter of English liberties, the Magna Carta of 1215. The constitutional conflicts between the English Crown and Parliament in the seventeenth century inspired a renewal of the declaratory urge, as Parliament forced Charles I to accept a Petition of Right in 1628 and then insisted that the newly crowned William and Mary agree to a Bill of Rights in 1689. These documents reaffirmed the "ancient rights and liberties" of Englishmen as represented in English common law and the customary relations between Crown and Parliament; they grew out of English legal traditions and constitutional quarrels rather than a universal human rights philosophy.[14] Locke's writings, forged in the midst of these very English struggles, helped turn the idea of rights and liberties in a more universalistic direction.

The idea of proclaiming a bill of rights passed over into the rebellious American colonies in the 1770s, where several state legislatures drew up such bills when they wrote new state constitutions. The most influential of these was the Virginia Bill of Rights, drafted by George Mason and adopted in 1776. It clearly influenced the French deputies when they met in 1789. The first article of the Virginia Bill of Rights held "That all men are by nature equally free and independent, and have certain inherent rights . . . namely, the enjoyment of life and liberty, with the means of acquiring and possessing property, and pursuing and obtaining happiness and safety." Like Jefferson's Declaration of Independence, the Virginia Bill of Rights proclaimed the rights of *all* men, not just Americans or Virginians. The new U.S. Congress began its discussion of a federal bill of rights at about the same time as the deputies in the new French National Assembly considered drafting a declaration of their own. The idea of making a solemn declaration of rights was definitely in the air.[15]

On June 17, 1789, after six weeks of inconclusive debate about voting procedures, the deputies of the Third Estate proclaimed themselves the true representatives of the nation; they invited the deputies from the two other orders to join them as deputies of a National Assembly. By the stroke of a pen—once the deputies of the clergy and the nobility began to join them—the Third Estate had transformed the political situation of the country, and as the National Assembly it turned to writing a constitution based on new principles. Many believed that the constitution must be preceded by a declaration of rights. Marquis de Lafayette, one of the most celebrated French participants in the American War of Independence and a close friend of Thomas Jefferson, offered the first proposal on July 11, 1789 (see Document 11).

Events quickly overtook the discussion. On July 13 the people of Paris learned that Louis XVI had secretly fired his finance minister Jacques Necker, a supporter of the Third Estate. Bands of Parisians began to arm themselves. On July 14 an armed crowd attacked the most imposing symbol of royal power in the city of Paris, the huge Bastille prison. When the garrison capitulated, the crowd cut off the head of the prison governor and paraded it through the streets. Parisians acted because they feared that the movement of thousands of army troops into their city presaged an attack on the new National Assembly, which met nearby in Versailles. The king had to back away from any such plan, if indeed he had one. The old leaders, from the king on down, began to lose their authority. Discussion of a declaration of rights now took place in a much tenser and more uncertain atmosphere, but it seemed, if anything, more urgent than ever.

When debate focused in August on the declaration (see Documents 12 and 13) it revealed a great diversity of opinion about the desirability of making any kind of proclamation of specific rights. This division of opinion continued down to the present; did the proclamation of rights provide the only viable basis for the government's legitimacy, or did it only create unreasonable expectations in a society that could not immediately deliver on the promise of equality? The influence of American models made itself felt in the discussion, but the French deputies clearly aimed for something even more universal: As Duke Mathieu de Montmorency exhorted, "[the Americans] have set a great example in the new hemisphere; let us give one to the universe." Even at this very early stage of discussion, the connection between natural rights and democracy as a form of government had already emerged; some argued that democracy might be suitable to the Americans with their custom of equality (Document 13) but could not be introduced in France, with its heritage of feudalism and aristocratic privilege.

Prominent deputies, including Abbé Sieyès and Marquis de Lafayette, rushed their proposed declarations into print for all to consider. In the end, however, the National Assembly adopted as its text for debate a compromise document drawn up collectively by one of its own subcommittees. In the ensuing discussion, the deputies modified and pared down the subcommittee's original twenty-four articles to seventeen. After six days of debate (August 20–24 and August 26), they voted to postpone any further discussion until after drawing up a new constitution. They never reopened the question. Thus the declaration (see Document 14) comprised the seventeen articles that could be agreed on during those six days of debate.

However much the subject of political negotiation and compromise at the time, the declaration exercised an enduring influence on all subsequent discussions of human rights. Like the Declaration of Independence and the Virginia Bill of Rights of 1776, the Declaration of the Rights of Man and Citizen spoke the language of "the natural, inalienable and sacred rights of man." But unlike its predecessors, it stood as the preamble to the constitution and provided the principles of political legitimacy. In the United States the Bill of Rights served to protect citizens from government and was composed only after the constitution itself was ratified; in France the declaration of rights provided the basis for government itself and was consequently drafted before the constitution.

The Declaration of the Rights of Man and Citizen laid out a vision of government based on principles completely different from those of the monarchy. According to the declaration, the legitimacy of government must now flow from the guarantee of individual rights by the law. Under the monarchy, legitimacy depended on the king's will and his maintenance of a historic order that granted privileges according to rank and status. Most remarkably, the deputies of 1789 endeavored to make a statement of universal application, rather than one particularly or uniquely French, and it is that universality that has ensured the continuing resonance of the document. In 1793 and again in 1795 new assemblies drew up new declarations, but these never enjoyed the prestige or authority of the 1789 declaration.

DEBATES OVER CITIZENSHIP AND RIGHTS DURING THE REVOLUTION

Rather than ending debate about rights, the vote on the declaration opened it up in new ways. The very existence of an official document based on universal principles seemed to encourage further consideration. Once the principle of rights and their guarantee as the basis of government had passed into law, a crucial question shaped succeeding discussions: Who was included in the definition of a "man and citizen"? The poor, the propertyless, religious minorities, blacks, mulattoes (people of mixed race), even women? Where should the lines be drawn? The question of citizenship helped drive the Revolution into increasingly radical directions after 1789 as one excluded group after another began to assert its claims.

The same issues about citizenship aroused debate and provoked political conflict in every Western democracy in the centuries that followed. It remains one of the most important problems, albeit in different forms, in democracies today. Should illegal immigrants, for example, have the same rights as citizens? How long must you reside in a country to merit citizenship and full rights? How old must you be to become a full citizen? And what counts as rights: access to housing, employment, a minimum wage, abortion, or even the right to die when you choose? The variety of these modern questions shows that once rights became the basis of legitimate government, debate would inevitably shift in new directions to consider who could exercise rights and what those rights might include.

French legislators approached the question of citizenship step by step over a period of five years after 1789. Rights became the subject of so much explicit discussion in France because the political situation remained fluid—at times violently unstable—during those years. Between 1789 and 1791 the National Assembly drafted legislation to establish a constitutional monarchy. To qualify for voting, men had to be property owners, but the deputies eliminated all the previous forms of legal privilege, including noble titles. An elected Legislative Assembly subsequently took office on October 1, 1791. The situation did not stabilize in 1791, however, in part because the king tried to flee to the border in disguise, in part because large numbers of former nobles left the country to form armies to combat the revolutionaries.

War brought political conflicts to a head. In April 1792, France went to war with Austria (seen as an instigator of counterrevolutionary efforts) and soon lost a series of critical battles. Faced with the threat of foreign invasion, a popular uprising in Paris on August 10, 1792, forced the Legislative Assembly to depose the king from his position. The "second revolution" of August 10 opened a much more radical period in French politics. The voters elected new deputies, who promptly abolished the monarchy and established a republic. Meeting as a National Convention, the deputies tried the king for treason and ordered his execution.

The fledgling republic faced an increasingly broad and desperate war with all the major European powers, most of them monarchies deeply suspicious of republican or democratic forms of government. Between September 1792 and the election of yet another government in 1795, the National Convention ruled by a combination of laws and emergency decrees. It suppressed property qualifications for voting and eventually abolished slavery in the French colonies, but at the same time it forbade women to set up their own political clubs, established new forms of censorship, and repressed most forms of political dissent. Under a regime known as the Terror, which lasted until the end of July 1794, revolutionary tribunals sentenced thousands of opponents of the government, male and female, to death at the newly invented guillotine. Rights and revolution therefore had a paradoxical relationship: The emergency government extended some rights in new directions (abolishing slavery) while violently suppressing others (especially freedom of speech).

After 1795, when another, still republican, constitution came into force, the political situation began to steady in some respects. The government used the guillotine much less frequently to terrorize its opponents, and it tried to rule by law rather than emergency decree. The discussion of rights, however, had reached its end; the new legislature considered turning back the clock on some issues (the deputies discussed revising or even abrogating the right to divorce made into law in 1792, for instance), but legislators found themselves too bogged down in ongoing political divisions to act decisively. Royalists wanted to reestablish the monarchy and bring back the nobility; left-wing republicans wanted to revive the political fervor of 1792–1794; right-wing republicans wanted a more authoritarian form of government with strong central leadership.

In 1799, General Napoleon Bonaparte seized his opportunity in the midst of this uncertainty and took charge of an entirely new government that turned in an increasingly authoritarian, militaristic direction. In 1802 he reestablished slavery in the French colonies, and in 1804 his new Civil Code relegated women to a legally inferior status. Throughout his regime he strictly controlled the press and other publications. The glory of the nation now took precedence over the rights of the individual, although Bonaparte did guarantee freedom of religion, access to official positions based on merit, and equality before the law.

Human rights philosophy had helped to undermine the traditional monarchy, and it provided the legitimacy of the revolutionary regimes. The Declaration of the Rights of Man and Citizen announced universal principles supposedly applicable to every individual in the nation (if not in the world). The very force of its universalistic logic seemed to support, if not positively provoke, growing demands for inclusion in the political process (at least until 1794). Thus it helped push the Revolution into radical directions, but it did not by itself afford a permanent foundation for rule. There are at least two ways of looking at this predicament: Some argue that the declaration was basically sound but too far ahead of its time, that the principle of human rights gained adherents only slowly over the course of the nineteenth and twentieth centuries and is not even fully subscribed to today; others insist that the declaration and human rights philosophy itself are inherently flawed because they are too universalistic and too abstract, too out of touch with the realities of human motivation, which depend more on self-interest, religious belief, nationality, or other forms of difference distinguishing groups of people. Moreover, guarantees of rights could all too easily be sacrificed when internal division or war threatened national security.

The collection of documents in this text cannot definitively resolve all these issues, but it can show how the discussion of rights developed during the French Revolution. The debates about citizenship fall into four major categories: the poor and the propertied; religious minorities; free blacks and slaves; and women. Not surprisingly, these are all in some sense social categories because most debates concerned the social qualifications necessary for citizenship. What is remarkable about this list is its extensiveness; no other eighteenth-century polity, not even the North Americans of the new United States, so explicitly discussed the rights of such a diversity of people. In the United States, for example, the question of women's rights hardly arose in public; there were no women's political clubs in the United States agitating for greater female participation and no public defenders of women's political rights among American legislators. Any discussion of women's rights in the eighteenth-century United States took place outside the halls of the legislature.

The French debates over citizenship and rights reveal a recurring clash between the ideals of human rights philosophy and the reality of eighteenth-century prejudices. Slaves, Jews, and women—to cite the most obvious examples—enjoyed political rights nowhere in the world in the eighteenth century. The mere discussion of their rights in a public forum was a novelty. What we should take from these debates, therefore, is not a sense of the backwardness of eighteenth-century views— what we would now call racism, anti-Semitism, and sexism were all very much alive and well at the time—but amazement at how many such issues French legislators felt they must publicly discuss, debate, and decide. The same prejudices shaped political life everywhere in the world at the time; what was new was the growing sentiment among French revolutionaries that changes must be made in the status of previously excluded groups.

The Poor and the Propertied

The decision to impose property qualifications for voting and holding office commanded nearly unanimous assent at first but came under attack not long afterward. The issue arose almost immediately in 1789; discussion of it had already begun during the debates over the declaration and had been prefigured in Sieyès's pamphlet on the Third Estate. The vast majority of the deputies who met in 1789 based their ideas on Locke and eighteenth-century political writers, who thought of citizenship and property holding as necessarily linked. They voted to establish a constitutional distinction between "active" and "passive" citizens, that is, between those who could vote and hold office (political rights) and those who enjoyed equal protection under the law in matters of marriage, property, or religion (civil rights) but could not participate directly in forming a government or exercising governmental authority.

Abbé Sieyès, who had argued forcefully for the elimination of the privileges of the nobility and the clergy, himself first proposed the active-passive distinction in July 1789 (see Document 15). Sieyès and the other deputies saw no inconsistency in their actions; they believed that all posts should be open to people with talent, but that potential officeholders first had to prove their worth by doing well enough to own property (see Document 16). Only a few deputies denounced the decision as incompatible with the declaration (see Document 17).

It is a measure of the rapid changes taking place in attitudes that this decision, once considered obvious, before long provoked discontent. The second revolution of August 10, 1792, forced the Legislative Assembly to abolish the active-passive distinction and grant the vote to all men except servants and the unemployed. The Constitution of 1793 (passed by the National Convention and ratified by popular referendum but shelved until the end of the war and hence never put into operation) admitted even servants to the full rights of citizenship, but the Constitution of 1795 excluded them once again. Debates over the status of servants, the propertyless, and the poor continued in France and elsewhere in the Western world throughout the nineteenth century and were not definitely resolved until the twentieth.

Religious Minorities and Questionable Professions

In December 1789 the deputies began to debate the unresolved status of non-Catholics (see Document 18). It quickly emerged that some assumed that the declaration automatically included all Protestants while others did not. In southern France, which had several numerous and wealthy Calvinist communities, the prospect of conceding political rights to Calvinists aroused strong feelings. Catholics in the city of Nîmes, for example, openly opposed granting political rights to Calvinists, in part because rich Calvinist merchants controlled local textile manufacturing. One anonymous pamphlet published there in October 1789 denounced the plots and secret maneuvers of the Calvinists, claiming that "the spirit of Calvinism is a spirit of independence, plunder, intolerance, injustice and inhumanity." The author insisted that the Catholics of the region "never intended to give their deputies the right to submit them to the despotism of their cruelest enemies."[16] Economic and political rivalries between the competing religious groups exploded in violent street-fighting in June 1790. Some three hundred people died, most of them Catholics.

As soon as the issue of Protestants arose, it sparked debate about the status of Jews, actors, and executioners—what to us now seems an unlikely combination! If religion was no barrier to citizenship in the case of Protestants, how could it be in the case of Jews? And why should one's profession be a disqualification for citizenship if the profession was legal? The status of Jews proved much more divisive than that of Calvinists, whose civil rights had already been guaranteed by the monarchy in the Edict of Toleration of 1787 (Document 3). The debates about the Jews are fascinating because they reveal the clash between long-standing prejudices and the new abstract principles of the declaration. If diversity of religious adherence was now allowed, how could religious affiliation be grounds for denying political rights?

Unlike the Protestants, the Jews did not seem to be automatically French, because many Jews did not speak French and their social customs differed in many ways from those of the French communities surrounding them. People who favored full citizenship for Jews did so on the grounds that Jews would no longer enjoy any separate status (they had their own corporative organization and paid separate taxes, for example).[17] As Count Stanislas Marie Adélaide de Clermont Tonnerre insisted, "We must refuse everything to the Jews as a nation and accord everything to Jews as individuals" (see Document 19). The Jews could no longer be a nation within the nation. They had to assimilate to the French nation and give up their separate status and identity if they were to participate as individual citizens like other French people. The deputies who believed that Jews should enjoy all political and civil rights also insisted that French nationality must be exactly the same for everyone; there could be, in essence, no specifically Jewish identity. The Jews, too, must become French. The majority of deputies, however, refused any immediate action; they voted to table the question of Jewish rights and leave it for future consideration (see Document 20).

Actors and executioners fared better than the Jews in the debates of December 1789. They had been excluded from holding local offices before 1789 because they practiced disreputable professions, but now the deputies agreed, despite some feeble opposition, that a man's profession could not disqualify him from rights that applied inherently to all men. These initial discussions showed that the question of rights could not be easily settled; if rights were universal, then boundaries or limits on their enjoyment required a lot of explanation. Once raised as an issue, moreover, the question of rights always aroused immediate reactions from the groups concerned (see Document 21 for the reactions of the actors themselves).

The postponement in December 1789 of any decision on the status of Jews had unforeseen results. The decision not to decide in effect took away rights already granted de facto to Jews of Spanish and Portuguese descent living in the south of France, for they, unlike Jews in the east, had already participated in the preliminary assemblies and elections for the Estates General and fully expected to continue participating on an equal footing in the new order. The Jews of the south met and chose a delegation to Paris to plead their case, and on January 28, 1790, the National Assembly declared that Portuguese and Spanish Jews would continue to enjoy their *previous* rights and by that virtue would qualify as active citizens if they met the other requirements.

At the same time, the Jews of Paris and the eastern regions prepared their own case for enjoying full rights of citizenship (see Document 22). They knew that the Jews of the south were presenting their requests to the National Assembly and hoped that their situation would be regulated in the same fashion, even though they had not enjoyed the same rights before the Revolution as the Jews of the south. They insisted in no uncertain terms "that all the degrading distinctions that they have suffered to this day be abolished and that they be declared CITIZENS." The deputies turned down their request.

Opposition to Jewish emancipation came from many quarters but had its most obvious sources in the eastern provinces of Alsace and Lorraine, with their thousands of Jews of eastern European heritage. Peasant riots against the Jews broke out in many eastern villages in the summer of 1789; peasants singled out those who had loaned them money. These disturbances continued sporadically in 1790 and 1791 and helped justify legislative inaction. Bishop Anne Louis Henri La Fare of the eastern town of Nancy spoke against Jewish rights in the December 1789 debate in the National Assembly and then published his speech as a pamphlet (see Document 23). His arguments were typical: The Jews were a foreign tribe to whom the French owed protection but not political rights. Moreover, he insisted, bestowing rights on the Jews would only inflame sentiment against them.

Nonetheless, the National Assembly finally acted in favor of the Jews on September 27, 1791. When a deputy introduced the decisive yet very simple motion (see Document 24), it passed with little discussion. It did include, however, a clause declaring that taking the civic oath "will be regarded as a renunciation of all the privileges and exceptions introduced previously in their [the Jews'] favor." In other words, Jews had to specifically renounce their privileges as a separate group in order to enjoy the rights of an individual, French citizen. French national identity had to take precedence over any other ethnic identification.

The tortured history of political rights for Jews illuminates the subterranean workings of human rights ideology. When Jewish emancipation was first suggested, many, if not most, deputies followed their time-worn prejudices and resisted the idea, arguing that at the least they needed more time and more facts to make an informed decision. Yet as time passed and the principles of human rights gained more adherents, at least among the educated elite, official discrimination against a religious group increasingly seemed incompatible with the Declaration of the Rights of Man and Citizen. This evolution shows that the meaning of "the rights of man" was not fixed at the beginning, even among men. It was instead the subject of intense and ever-changing debate. The direction of movement was clear, however; limitations on rights proved harder and harder to justify.

Free Blacks and Slaves

The debates over free blacks and slaves followed an even more zigzag course than those over religion. Most deputies feared the effects of the loss of commerce that would result from either the abolition of slavery or the elimination of the slave trade. Fabulous wealth depended on slavery; shipbuilding, sugar refining, coffee consumption, and a host of subsidiary industries rested on the slave trade, and slaveowners and shippers did not intend to give up their prospects without a fight. The United States' refusal to give up slavery or the slave trade provided added ammunition for their position. The Society of the Friends of Blacks continued to agitate in favor of either limitation or abolition of the slave trade, but it and its supporters came under intense attack for their views. As a result, early proposals, especially those for the abolition of slavery (as opposed to the slave trade), had an almost apologetic tone (see Document 25).

Events in France had not gone unnoticed in the colonies. When the white planters of Saint Domingue, the wealthiest French colony in the Caribbean, sent delegates to France to demand their representation at the new National Assembly, the mulattoes of the colony promptly dispatched representatives to demand their inclusion too. On the eve of the Revolution, Saint Domingue had 500,000 slaves, 30,000 whites, and 28,000 free blacks, a category that included both blacks and mulattoes. Some free blacks owned slaves; in fact, free blacks owned one-third of the plantation property and one-quarter of the slaves in Saint Domingue, although they could not hold public office or practice many professions (such as medicine). Vincent Ogé, a mulatto lawyer and slaveowner, presented the views of the mulatto delegates to the white planters who had come to Paris (see Document 26); he hoped to convince them that they shared many interests as property owners in the colonies. White and mulatto planters both wanted representation in France but also wished to maintain control of their slaves. Ogé's appeal failed, for the white planters feared that any concession on the matter of color would open a fatal crack in the slave system.

Several prominent deputies in the National Assembly belonged to the Society of the Friends of Blacks, including Grégoire and Lafayette. Faced with determined opposition to the abolition of either the slave trade or slavery, many deputies favorable to blacks turned instead to arguing that full civil and political rights be granted to free blacks in the colonies. Grégoire spoke in the National Assembly on the subject of mulatto rights in October 1789 and published a pamphlet in their favor (see Document 27). Confronted with growing hostility to their position in the National Assembly, especially on the part of those sympathetic to the fears of the planters in the colonies, the Society of the Friends of Blacks retreated from any suggestion that slavery be abolished and instead argued for the abolition of the slave trade (see Document 28).

The agitation in favor of granting rights to free blacks and abolishing the slave trade created uncertainty in the colonies and raised expectations, especially among free blacks and mulattoes. In response, white planters mounted their own counterattack and even began to contemplate demanding independence from France. Less is known about the views of the slaves because most could not read or write, but the royal governor of Saint Domingue expressed his worries about the effects of the Revolution on them. In October 1789 he reported that the slaves considered the new revolutionary cockade (a decoration made up of red, white, and blue ribbons worn by supporters of the Revolution) as a "signal of the manumission of the whites . . . the blacks all share an idea that struck them spontaneously: that the white slaves killed their masters and now free they govern themselves and regain possession of the land."[18] In other words, black slaves hoped to follow in the footsteps of their white predecessors, freeing themselves, killing their masters, and taking the land.

To quiet the unrest among the powerful white planters, especially in Saint Domingue, the colonial committee of the National Assembly proposed in March 1790 to exempt the colonies from the constitution and to prosecute anyone who attempted to prompt uprisings against the slave system (see Document 29). But steadily increasing unrest threatened the efforts of the National Assembly to mollify the white planters and keep a lid on racial tensions. The March 1790 decree said nothing about the political rights of free blacks, who continued to press their demands both in Paris and back home, but to no avail. In October 1790, Ogé led a rebellion of 350 mulattoes in Saint Domingue. French army troops cooperated with local planter militias to disperse and arrest them. In February 1791, Ogé and other mulatto leaders were publicly executed. Nevertheless, on May 15,1791, under renewed pressure from Grégoire and others, the National Assembly granted political rights to all free blacks and mulattoes who were born of free mothers and fathers; although this proviso limited rights to a few hundred free blacks, the white colonists furiously pledged to resist the application of the law. Then, on August 22, 1791, the slaves of Saint Domingue began what was to become over the next several years the first successful slave revolt in history. In response, the National Assembly rescinded the rights of free blacks and mulattoes on September 24, 1791, prompting them once again to take up arms against the whites.

Fighting continued as the new Legislative Assembly (it replaced the National Assembly in October 1791) considered free black rights again at the end of March 1792 (see Document 30). On March 28 the assembly voted to reinstate the political rights of free blacks and mulattoes. Nothing was done about slavery. In the fall of 1792, as the Revolution in mainland France began to radicalize, the French government sent two agents to Saint Domingue to take charge of the suppression of the slave revolt. Faced with the prospect of British and Spanish invasions aimed at taking over the colony with the aid of the rebel slaves, the agents instead abolished slavery in the colony (August–October 1793). Although the National Convention initially denounced their actions as part of a conspiracy to aid Great Britain, it finally voted to abolish slavery in all the French colonies on February 4, 1794 (see Document 31). Many mulattoes opposed this move because they owned slaves themselves.

For all the deputies' good intentions, however, the situation remained confused in almost all the colonies: Some local authorities simply disregarded the decree; others converted slavery into forced labor; others were too busy fighting the British and Spanish to decide one way or the other. In 1802, Napoleon Bonaparte reestablished slavery and the slave trade and denied political rights to free blacks. In Saint Domingue, however, the former slaves continued their revolt, and in 1804 they established the independent republic of Haiti.

Women

Although the cause of women's rights gained less support than other rights issues, some did see it as essential. The antislavery activist Condorcet published a newspaper article on women's political rights in July 1790 (see Document 32). In it he argued that the twelve million French women should enjoy equal political rights with men. In his view, rights were inherent in personhood; "either no individual in mankind has true rights, or all have the same ones." He refuted many of the traditional arguments against women, insisting that education and social conditions produced most of the differences between men and women. But his pleas fell for the most part on deaf ears. None of the national assemblies ever considered legislation granting political rights to women (who could neither vote nor hold office), and on the few occasions on which the possibility arose, however tentatively, the deputies greeted it with widespread derision and incredulity.

Still, a small band of supporters of women's rights did take shape. They met in a group called the *Cercle Social* (social circle), which launched a campaign for women's rights in 1790–1791. One of their most active members in the area of women's rights was the Dutch woman Etta Palm d'Aelders (see Document 33), who denounced the prejudices against women that denied them equal rights in marriage and in education. Like many female activists, she did not explicitly articulate a program for equal political rights for women, although that would no doubt have been her ultimate aim. Instead she worked to bring about a change in morals and customs that would in turn foster a more egalitarian atmosphere for women. In their newspapers and pamphlets, the Cercle Social, whose members later became ardent republicans, argued for a liberal divorce law and reforms in inheritance laws as well. Their associated political club set up a female section in March 1791 to work specifically on women's issues, including lobbying for civil equality in the areas of divorce and property.[19]

The Cercle Social was not alone in agitating for women's rights. One of the most striking statements of women's rights came from the pen of Marie Gouze, better known by her pen name Olympe de Gouges. An aspiring playwright, Gouges bitterly attacked the slave system and in September 1791 published a Declaration of the Rights of Woman (see Document 34) modeled on the Declaration of the Rights of Man and Citizen. She closely followed the structure and language of the Declaration of the Rights of Man and Citizen in order to show how women had been excluded from its promises. Her Article 1, for example, proclaimed that "Woman is born free and remains equal to man in rights." Article 6 insisted that "The law should be the expression of the general will. All citizenesses and citizens should take part . . . in its formation. It must be the same for everyone. All citizenesses and citizens, being equal in its eyes, should be equally admissible to all public dignities, offices and employments." In short, she argued that women should have all the rights that men enjoyed, including the right to hold public office. Although her declaration did not garner widespread support, it did make her notorious. Like many other leading female activists, she suffered persecution at the hands of the government. Etta Palm d'Aelders and most of the others had to endure only arrest, however; Gouges went to the guillotine in 1793. One of the leaders of the Paris city government denounced her as a "shameless" woman who "abandoned the cares of her household to involve herself in the republic" (Document 38). Public political activism came at a high price.

Although the various legislative assemblies refused to grant women equal political rights, demands for such rights created ripples of discussion in political circles. In February 1791 a major Parisian newspaper responded explicitly to women's demands and to the men, especially Condorcet, who had spoken in their favor (see Document 35). In his editorial, Louis Prudhomme developed in embryonic form the argument that would be used against women in official circles thereafter: Women's social role was to stay home, raise the family, instill private virtues, and stay out of public affairs. When the deputies discussed a new republican constitution in April 1793, however, arguments could still be heard in favor of equal political rights for women (see Document 36). The official spokesman for the constitutional committee recognized the existence of disagreement on this question and cited in particular the treatise by Pierre Guyomar, a deputy close to the members of the Cercle Social, who defended the political equality of the sexes in the strongest of terms. Guyomar maintained that the "man" in the Declaration of the Rights of Man was generic; it applied to both men and women. He insisted that men should liberate themselves from the prejudice of sex just as they had liberated themselves from the prejudice "against the color of Negroes."

Guyomar failed to convince his fellow deputies, but women persisted in fashioning political roles for themselves (see Figure 1). In May 1793 a group of Parisian women founded an exclusively female political club, the Society of Revolutionary Republican Women. They did not explicitly discuss the right to vote or hold office in their meetings, but they did agitate for the establishment of armed military groups of women and for sterner measures against opponents of the Revolution. By this time, France faced not only a war on several fronts abroad but also a civil war at home between the republic and its opponents who had raised armies in western France. Subversion from within seemed at least as dangerous as enemy armies on the frontiers. Women in the provinces founded some sixty clubs of their own; they established charity workshops for the production of blankets and bandages for the war effort, helped orchestrate local festivals, lobbied for local price controls, defended the clergy who supported the Revolution, and repeatedly petitioned the National Convention on political and economic questions.[20]

The activities of the Paris women's club soon gained the unfavorable attention of the National Convention, and after a brief discussion (see Document 37) the deputies voted on October 30, 1793, to suppress all women's clubs. According to the spokesman Jean-Baptiste Amar, women "are hardly capable of lofty conceptions and serious cogitations." Their biology and their social role, as Prudhomme had argued two years earlier, made them unsuited for public affairs. Pierre-Gaspard Chaumette reiterated these views several days later when a deputation of women appeared at the Paris city hall wearing red caps as a symbol of liberty (see Document 38). Public activity by women, in his view, amounted to nothing less than a renunciation of their sex.

Thus, not long before the National Convention voted to abolish slavery and a full two years after a previous legislature had granted full political rights to Jewish men, the deputies resolutely rejected not only political rights for women but even their right to engage in any form of organized politics. Before concluding too hastily, however, that the French Revolution was simply "bad for women," one should recognize that women played a more active role in the French Revolution than in any other comparable political movement of the eighteenth century. They formed their own clubs and also agitated in print and in mixed-sex

Figure 1. Titled "You Will Be Happy," this is one of the rare engravings known to be from the hand of a woman, Citizeness Rollet. Rollet presumably was sympathetic to the abolition of slavery. Her engraving is an example of women's ability to participate in politics without having the right to vote.

clubs for more rights not only in politics but also in inheritance and marriage laws. In the American (1776) and Dutch (1787) revolutions, women sometimes formed clubs but never for explicit political purposes; they devoted themselves exclusively to philanthropic and auxiliary activities. Only in France during the French Revolution did women (or men) make explicit demands for full female political equality. In other words, even though the National Convention clamped down on women's political activities, it did so only after the demands for women's rights had been made. Once made, such demands did not disappear, and the woman question would emerge again in future revolutionary situations, not only in France but elsewhere. The women's rights movement of the nineteenth and twentieth centuries could trace its origins to the French Revolution because the French Revolution, more than any other event of its time, opened up the question of women's rights for consideration.

The "rights of man" was a relatively new political concept in 1789, and the leaders of the French Revolution, like those of the American Revolution before them, were not always comfortable with its implications. However discomfited, French legislators granted more far-reaching rights than any such body ever had before. Like the Americans, the French revolutionaries refused equal political rights to women, but unlike the Americans, they voted to abolish slavery and the slave trade and eventually granted equal rights, at least in principle, to all men regardless of wealth, color, or religion. Americans at that time did not abolish slavery or the slave trade, despite many voices urging abolition, and since voting qualifications remained under the jurisdiction of the states in the new United States, states could maintain property qualifications and religious tests (and most did) for citizenship.[21] Yet despite these differences, the French and the Americans had one important thing in common: They both officially declared the equality of rights—with whatever real legal impediments—as part of their revolutions. They gave birth to an idea that would make slow but steady progress in Europe and the rest of the world during the nineteenth and twentieth centuries.

NATIONAL SECURITY AND LIMITS ON RIGHTS

Rights guaranteed under the law sometimes represented more of an aspiration than a practical reality. Rioting and intimidation kept Protestants in the south of France and Jews in the east from full and immediate political participation, and deep uncertainty plagued the official emancipation of the slaves in the French colonies. Moreover, the deputies brought eighteenth-century assumptions to their new political order, and these assumptions sometimes stood in the way of individual rights. Even before the outbreak of the Revolution, Sieyès had articulated the widely shared view that nothing should stand between the individual and the nation (Document 10): "Anybody who holds a legal privilege of any kind," he wrote, "leaves [the] common order, [and] stands as an exception to the common law." He had in mind the nobles, but during the Revolution such thinking applied as well to trade associations and even the idea of a political party (which by its very name suggests a division of the whole). As deputy Isaac Le Chapelier explained in presenting a law of 1791 against trade associations (see Document 39), "there is only the particular interest of each individual and the general interest. No one is allowed to inspire an intermediate interest among citizens." He argued that trade associations were incompatible with free trade and the public interest. French workers gained the right to strike only in 1864 and the right to unionize in 1884.

When the revolutionary government encountered resistance to its reforms of the Catholic Church, it began to take action against the Catholic clergy. Clerics who refused an oath of loyalty to the new regime were deprived of their positions and later became subject to arrest, exile, and execution as counterrevolutionaries. In April 1792, the deputies voted to suppress religious organizations, even those devoted to charity work, and to prohibit the wearing of clerical vestments in public (see Document 40). More radical measures were yet to come. In addition to drawing up a new calendar making the foundation of the republic the inauguration of a new era (1792 became year one of the republic, and all the months were given new names taken from nature), the most radical republicans mounted a de-Christianization campaign to attack the prerogatives of the churches. Although the Catholic Church provided their most important target, the radical republicans also closed synagogues and Protestant churches, burned Protestant and Jewish religious books, exiled recalcitrant rabbis and pastors, and confiscated religious objects of all sorts for the use of the nation. The government soon disavowed the de-Christianization campaign, but the public display of religious affiliation remains an enduring subject of controversy in France.[22]

After France declared war on Austria in April 1792, the sense that the fatherland was in danger soon reached frightening proportions and intensified every time France faltered in fighting off a growing list of declared enemies, both within the country and without. Many people demanded more prompt and severe retribution against those suspected of aiding the enemy. Rumors of conspiracies and plots seemed all too believable after leading generals such as Lafayette defected to the enemy. In March 1793, the deputies established a special revolutionary court to hear cases in Paris. In September 1793, they voted a Law on Suspects (see Document 41) that opened the door to massive denunciations and arrests. Scholars still debate how many were arrested under this shockingly general set of categories, perhaps as many as 300,000 people. The chase after traitors seemed to take on a life of its own; several of the political figures featured in this volume were eventually accused of treason, and many died either by their own hand or at the guillotine. In June 1794, the deputies voted to limit the rights of defendants before the revolutionary court (see Document 42). Only two verdicts were allowed — acquittal or death — and defendants could not call upon lawyers to assist them. The law terrified many deputies, however, and within weeks they had organized to overthrow Robespierre and his followers, who were subsequently blamed for all the bloodletting.

Contemporary political life almost everywhere is now caught up in the language and practices of rights that had their first articulation in the late seventeenth and eighteenth centuries. Reading through the debates of the French Revolution, we gain a clearer sense not only of how people in the past viewed themselves and their "fellow men," but also of how we ourselves think about our political world.

NOTES

[1]The text of the declaration was approved on December 10, 1948 by the General Assembly of the United Nations. *Yearbook on Human Rights for 1948* (Lake Success, N.Y.: United Nations, 1950), 466.

[2]As quoted in Maurice Cranston, "Are There Any Human Rights?" *Daedalus* 112 (Fall 1983): 4.

[3]The best general history of the philosophical development of the modern concepts of human autonomy can be found in the difficult but rewarding book by Charles Taylor, *Sources of the Self: The Making of Modern Identity* (Cambridge, Mass.: Harvard University Press, 1989).

[4]John Locke, *Two Treatises of Government* (Cambridge: Cambridge University Press, 1963), 366–67.

[5]For a general account of shifts in opinion, see Geoffrey Adams, *The Huguenots and French Opinion, 1685–1787: The Enlightenment Debate on Toleration* (Waterloo, Ontario, Canada: Wilfrid Laurier University Press, 1991).

[6]Patrick Girard, *La Révolution française et les juifs* (Paris: Robert Laffont, 1989).

[7]Quotes from Arthur Hertzberg, *The French Enlightenment and the Jews* (New York: Columbia University Press, 1968), 280, 302–3. Hertzberg tends to read Voltaire (and everyone else he reads) out of context, however, so as to exaggerate his case for the anti-Semitism of Enlightenment thinkers.

[8]Girard, *La Révolution française,* 81.

[9]Hertzberg considers Zalkind Hourwitz, the one Jewish respondent and one of the winners of the Metz essay contest, to be anti-Semitic, at least in his hatred of rabbis. This

seems to me to be all too typical of Hertzberg's anachronistic way of reading out of historical context; he applies a twentieth-century, post-Holocaust standard of judgment to eighteenth-century writers, making little effort to understand what they might have meant in their own time. By this kind of standard just about everyone writing in the eighteenth century was racist, sexist, and/or anti-Semitic, and thus all distinction between positions is lost. Hertzberg, *The French Enlightenment*, 335. For a more balanced treatment, see Ronald Schechter, *Obstinate Hebrews: Representations of Jews in France, 1715–1815* (Berkeley: University of California Press, 2003).

[10]"Sodomie," in *Oeuvres complètes de Condorcet*, ed. D. J. Garat and P. J. G. Cabanis, 21 vols. (Paris: Ch. Fr. Cramer, 1802), 7:374. Condorcet considered sodomy "a low, disgusting vice," but he did not believe that it should be punished by the law. Revolutionary legislators left it out of their new criminal code proposed in 1791, but they did not engage in a public discussion of the question, so we have little evidence for their views.

[11]For a useful account of the differences between the two societies, see James Dybikowski, "Slavery, Revolution and Political Strategy: Lessons from the International Campaign to Abolish the Slave Trade," *Lumen: Selected Proceedings from the Canadian Society for Eighteenth-Century Studies* 13 (1994): 87–98.

[12]Joan Kelly, "Early Feminist Theory and the Querelle des Femmes, 1480–1789," *Signs* 8 (1982): 4–28.

[13]A detailed study of a region in the Southwest of France has shown that women appeared in small numbers at many parish meetings to participate in the election of delegates and the drafting of grievance lists. This probably reflected local customs, which held in some places, for example, that women could participate in parish assemblies if they were heads of family or held property in the district. Women seem to have participated in small numbers all across France, in part because the electoral regulations were vague on many points. They did not meet anywhere as a separate group. René Larivière, "Le Vote des femmes à la Révolution," in *Le Périgord révolutionnaire: Le grand livre sur la Révolution en Périgord* (Périgueux: Société historique et archéologique du Périgord, 1989), 507–37.

[14]See Carl Stephenson and Frederick George Marcham, eds., *Sources of English Constitutional History*, rev. ed., 2 vols. (New York: Harper and Row, 1972).

[15]On the French origins of the idea of a declaration, see Keith Michael Baker, "The Idea of a Declaration of Rights," in *The French Idea of Freedom: The Old Regime and the Declaration of Rights of 1789*, ed. Dale Van Hey (Stanford, Calif.: Stanford University Press, 1994), 154–96.

[16]*Charles Sincère à Pierre Romain*, Nîmes, Oct. 22, 1789. This was an anonymous pamphlet written as a letter from one Catholic to another in Nîmes.

[17]A useful discussion of these issues can be found in Gary Kates, "Jews into Frenchmen: Nationality and Representation in Revolutionary France," *Social Research* 56 (1989): 213–32. Reprinted in *The French Revolution and the Birth of Modernity*, ed. Ferenc Fehér (Berkeley: University of California Press, 1990), 103–16.

[18]FR ANOM COL C9A 161, Correspondance générale Saint Domingue.

[19]Gary Kates, "'The Powers of Husband and Wife Must Be Equal and Separate': The Cercle Social and the Rights of Women, 1790–91," in *Women and Politics in the Age of the Democratic Revolution*, ed. Harriet B. Applewhite and Darline G. Levy (Ann Arbor: University of Michigan Press, 1990), 163–80.

[20]Suzanne Desan, "'Constitutional Amazons': Jacobin Women's Clubs in the French Revolution," in *Re-creating Authority in Revolutionary France*, ed. Bryant T. Ragan Jr. and Elizabeth A. Williams (New Brunswick, N.J.: Rutgers University Press, 1992), 11–35.

[21]See, for example, Stanley F. Chyet, "The Political Rights of Jews in the United States: 1776–1840," *American Jewish Archives* 10 (April 1958): 14–75.

[22]Joan Wallach Scott, *The Politics of the Veil* (Princeton, N.J.: Princeton University Press, 2007).

PART TWO

The Documents

1

Defining Rights before 1789

Natural Law as Defined by the *Encyclopedia*, 1755

1

DIDEROT

"Natural Law"

1755

The writers of the French Enlightenment made much of the concept of natural law or natural right (the French word droit *covers both meanings). As this selection from the* Encyclopedia *demonstrates, natural law provided the most basic foundation for all human society, that is, it defined what was naturally just for all humans, regardless of country or time period. Enlightenment writers focused on natural law as a way of criticizing particular French laws that they saw as incompatible with those more fundamental human rights. Our modern notion of human rights derives from this earlier notion of natural law or right, that sense of justice common to all peoples.*

When they initiated the project of compiling a French Encyclopedia, *Denis Diderot and Jean d'Alembert had various aims. They took on as collaborators all the well-known writers of the day, many of whom had been in trouble with the authorities in the past. Their proclaimed purpose*

Denis Diderot and Jean Le Rond d'Alembert, eds., *Encyclopédie ou Dictionnaire raisonné des sciences, arts, et des métiers*, 17 vols. (1751–1780), vol. 5 (Paris: Chez Briasson, 1755), 115–16.

was to present all the knowledge available to humankind in a form that could be readily passed on to future generations. But they also intended to use that knowledge as a means of challenging and reshaping the status quo. They believed that knowledge would lead inevitably to "enlightenment," that is, action based on reason rather than on superstition, bigotry, or religious fanaticism.

Diderot himself wrote this brief article, thereby underlining the importance of the concept. The article does not have the satirical bite of some of the others in the Encyclopedia, *yet careful reading uncovers a frontal challenge to the French legal order of the mid-eighteenth century. When grounding universal justice and the good society, natural law or right requires no reference to kings, aristocracy, or deference to one's social betters — indeed, to special privilege of any kind. The philosophy of natural law — and here its development into the eighteenth-century idea of the "general will" — implied legally equal individuals joining together in a society based only on universal human characteristics. Articles such as these immediately drew the attention of censors and police. The government and the Catholic Church both banned the* Encyclopedia *and persecuted its editors, but the commotion only attracted more readers to clandestine and pirated editions.*

NATURAL LAW. The use of this term is so familiar that there is almost no one who would not be convinced inside himself that the thing is obviously known to him. This interior feeling is common both to the philosopher and to the man who has not reflected at all. . . . [The article then advances a series of propositions.]

4. I see first of all one thing that seems to me to be acknowledged both by good and evil persons: that we must reason in everything because man is not simply an animal but an animal who reasons. There are consequently in the question at hand means for discovering the truth. Whoever refuses to look for the truth renounces human status and must be treated by the rest of his species like a ferocious beast; once the truth is discovered, whoever refuses to conform to it is either mad or bad in a moral sense. . . .

7. It is to the general will that the individual must address himself to learn how to be a man, citizen, subject, father, child, and when it is suitable to live or to die. It fixes the limits on all duties. You have the most sacred *natural right* to everything that is not disputed by the rest of the species. The general will enlightens you on the nature of your thoughts

and your desires. Everything that you conceive, everything that you meditate upon will be good, grand, elevated, sublime, if it is in the general and common interest. . . . Tell yourself often: I am a man, and I have no other true, inalienable *natural rights* than those of humanity.

8. But, you will say to me, where is this general will kept? Where can I consult it? In the principles of written law of all the organized nations; in the social actions of savage and barbarous peoples; in the tacit conventions held in common by the enemies of humankind; and even in indignation and resentment, those two passions that nature seems to have placed in all creatures including animals to make up for the shortcomings in social laws and in public vengeance.

9. If you meditate attentively therefore on everything said in the preceding, you will remain convinced 1) that the man who only listens to his private will is the enemy of the human race; 2) that in every individual the *general* will is a pure act of understanding that reasons in the silence of the passions about what man can demand of his fellow man and about what his fellow man has the right to demand of him; 3) that this attention to the general will of the species and to shared wants is the rule of conduct of one individual relative to another in the same society, of an individual toward the society of which he is a member, and of the society of which he is a member toward other societies; 4) that submission to the general will is the basis of all societies, without excepting those formed for crime. Indeed, virtue is so attractive that thieves respect its image even inside their dens! 5) that the laws should be made for everyone, and not for one person.

2

VOLTAIRE

Treatise on Toleration

1763

Voltaire was the pen name of François Marie Arouet (1694–1778), perhaps the single best-known writer of the Enlightenment. As early as 1723, he made a name for himself as a proponent of religious toleration when he published a long poem about French King Henry IV and the sixteenth-century wars of religion between Catholics and Calvinists (La Henriade). Visits to England and the Dutch Republic in the 1720s impressed on him the political benefits that could be reaped from religious pluralism. His involvement in the Calas Affair in the 1760s turned it into a European scandal. He wrote his treatise on toleration to link the Calas case to more general issues of religious freedom. He did not argue for granting political rights to members of every religion, but he did insist on the virtues of the freedom to practice one's chosen religion without persecution. He grounded this freedom on natural law. Even this was too much for French authorities, who promptly banned the work.

Short Account of the Death of Jean Calas

The murder of Calas, which was perpetrated with the sword of justice at Toulouse on March 9, 1762, is one of the most singular events that deserve the attention of our own and of later ages. We quickly forget the long list of the dead who have perished in our battles. It is the inevitable fate of war; those who die by the sword might themselves have inflicted death on their enemies, and did not die without the means of defending

---

Voltaire, *Toleration and Other Essays*, trans. Joseph McCabe (New York: G. P. Putnam's Sons, 1912), 1–2, 26–28, 30–31.

themselves. When the risk and the advantage are equal astonishment ceases, and even pity is enfeebled. But when an innocent father is given into the hands of error, of passion, or of fanaticism; when the accused has no defence but his virtue; when those who dispose of his life run no risk but that of making a mistake; when they can slay with impunity by a legal decree—then the voice of the general public is heard, and each fears for himself. They see that no man's life is safe before a court that has been set up to guard the welfare of citizens, and every voice is raised in a demand of vengeance. . . .

How Toleration May Be Admitted

I venture to think that some enlightened and magnanimous minister, some humane and wise prelate, some prince who puts his interest in the number of his subjects and his glory in their welfare, may deign to glance at this inartistic and defective paper. . .

We have Jews at Bordeaux and Metz and in Alsace; we have Lutherans, Molinists, and Jansenists; can we not suffer and control Calvinists on much the same terms as those on which Catholics are tolerated at London [who did not enjoy political rights but could practice their religion]? The more sects there are, the less danger in each. Multiplicity enfeebles them. They are all restrained by just laws which forbid disorderly meetings, insults, and sedition, and are ever enforced by the community.

We know that many fathers of families, who have made large fortunes in foreign lands, are ready to return to their country [the Calvinist refugees]. They ask only the protection of natural law, the validity of their marriages, security as to the condition of their children, the right to inherit from their fathers, and the enfranchisement of their persons. They ask not for public chapels, or the right to municipal offices and dignities. Catholics have not these things in England and other countries. It is not a question of giving immense privileges and secure positions to a faction, but of allowing a peaceful people to live, and of moderating the laws once, but no longer, necessary. It is not our place to tell the ministry what is to be done; we do but ask consideration for the unfortunate. . . .

The great means to reduce the number of fanatics, if any remain, is to submit that disease of the mind to the treatment of reason, which slowly, but infallibly, enlightens men. Reason is gentle and humane. It inspires liberality, suppresses discord, and strengthens virtue; it has more power to make obedience to the laws attractive than force has to compel. . . .

Whether Intolerance Is of Natural and Human Law

Natural law is that indicated to men by nature. . . . Human law must in every case be based on natural law. All over the earth the great principle of both is: Do not unto others what you would that they do not unto you. Now, in virtue of this principle, one man cannot say to another: "Believe what I believe, and what thou canst not believe, or thou shalt perish." Thus do men speak in Portugal, Spain, and Goa. In some other countries they are now content to say: "Believe, or I detest thee; believe, or I will do thee all the harm I can. Monster, thou sharest not my religion, and therefore hast no religion; thou shalt be a thing of horror to thy neighbours, thy city, and thy province."

If it were a point of human law to behave thus, the Japanese should detest the Chinese, who should abhor the Siamese; the Siamese, in turn, should persecute the Tibetans, who should fall upon the Hindus. A Mogul should tear out the heart of the first Malabarian he met; the Malabarian should slay the Persian, who might massacre the Turk; and all of them should fling themselves against the Christians, who have so long devoured each other.

The supposed right of intolerance is absurd and barbaric. It is the right of the tiger; nay, it is far worse, for tigers do but tear in order to have food, while we rend each other for paragraphs.

3

Edict of Toleration

November 1787

Calvinists had a long and tumultuous history in France. They first gained the right to worship according to their creed in 1598 when King Henry IV issued the Edict of Nantes to end the wars of religion between Catholics and Calvinists. Louis XIV revoked that edict in 1685 and initiated a massive campaign to forcibly convert all of the Calvinists in France.

Edit concernant ceux qui ne font pas profession de la religion catholique (Nov. 28, 1787), *Recueil général des anciennes lois françaises, depuis l'an 420 jusqu'à la Révolution de 1789*, ed. François André Isambert, 29 vols. (Paris: Belin-le-Prieur, 1821–1833), vol. 28, *Du 1er janvier 1785 au 5 mai 1789* (Paris, 1827), 472–82.

For more than a century, public worship by Calvinists remained illegal, although many worshiped in private and some became leading merchants or businessman in their local communities. Finally, in 1787, Louis XVI's government proposed a new edict of toleration (the decision became official in January 1788). It granted Calvinists civil rights, including the right to practice their religion, but no political rights. Although the reference to non-Catholics might seem to promise a broader toleration including other groups as well, the edict applied only to Calvinists, for Jewish and Lutheran communities were covered by separate legislation. The preamble to the edict, with its evasive and tormented logic, shows the many pressures felt by the government as it tried to navigate between the demands of a powerful Catholic Church and a long-oppressed minority that had the support of many influential writers and jurists.

When Louis XIV solemnly prohibited in all of the lands and territories under his authority the public exercise of any religion other than the Catholic religion, the hope of bringing around his people to the desirable unity of the same worship, supported by the deceptive appearances of conversions, kept this great king from following the plan that he had formed in his councils for legally registering the births, deaths, and marriages of those of his subjects who could not be admitted to the sacraments of the church. Following the example of our august predecessors, we will always favor with all our power the means of instruction and persuasion that will tend to link all our subjects by the common profession of our kingdom's ancient faith [Catholicism], and we will proscribe, with the most severe attention, all those violent routes [of forced conversion] which are as contrary to the principles of reason and humanity as they are to the true spirit of Christianity.

But, while waiting for divine Providence to bless our efforts and effect this happy revolution [the conversion of all non-Catholics], justice and the interest of our kingdom do not permit us to exclude any longer from the rights of civil status those of our subjects or resident foreigners in our empire who do not profess the Catholic religion. A rather long experience has shown that harsh ordeals are insufficient to convert them: we should therefore no longer suffer that our laws punish them unnecessarily for the misfortune of their birth by depriving them of the rights that nature constantly claims for them.

We have considered that the Protestants, thus deprived of all legal existence, were faced with an impossible choice between profaning the sacraments by simulated conversions or compromising the status of their children by contracting marriages that were inherently null and void according to the legislation of our kingdom. The regulations have even assumed that there were only Catholics in our states; and this fiction, today inadmissible, has served as a motive for the silence of the law which would not have been able to legally recognize followers of another belief in France without either banishing them from the lands of our authority or providing right away for their civil status. . . .

The Catholic religion that we have the good fortune to profess will alone enjoy in our kingdom the rights and honors of public worship, while our other, non-Catholic subjects, deprived of all influence on the established order in our state, declared in advance and forever ineligible for forming a separate body within our kingdom, and subject to the ordinary police [and not their own clergy] for the observation of religious festival days, will only get from the law what natural right does not permit us to refuse them, to register their births, their marriages, and their deaths, in order to enjoy, like all our other subjects, the civil effects that result from this.

Article 1.   The Catholic, Apostolic, and Roman religion will continue to enjoy alone, in our kingdom, the right to public worship, and the birth, marriage, and death of those of our subjects who profess it will only be registered, in all cases, according to the rites and practices of the said religion as authorized by our regulations.

We will permit nonetheless to those of our subjects who profess another religion than the Catholic, Apostolic, and Roman religion, whether they are currently resident in our state or establish themselves there afterwards, to enjoy all the goods and rights that currently can or will in the future belong to them as a property title or title of successorship, and to pursue their commerce, arts, crafts, and professions without being troubled or disturbed on the pretext of their religion.

We except nevertheless from these professions all the offices of the judiciary, controlled either by the crown or the *seigneurs* [nobles controlling local judicial offices], municipalities having regular offices and judicial functions, and all those places that include public teaching.

Article 2.   As a consequence those of our subjects or foreigners resident in our kingdom who are not of the Catholic religion will be able to contract marriages in the form hereafter prescribed; we wish these marriages and their children, in the case of those who contracted them according to the said form, to have the same effects in civil society as those contracted and celebrated in the ordinary way by our Catholic subjects.

Article 3. We do not intend nevertheless that those who will profess a religion other than the Catholic religion be able to consider themselves as forming in our kingdom any particular body, community or association, nor that they be able under such a designation to formulate any collective demands, make any representations, take any deliberations, make any acquisitions, or take any other such acts. We very expressly prohibit any judge, registrar, notary, lawyer, or other public official to respond, receive, or sign such demands, representations, deliberations or other acts on pain of suspension; and we forbid any of our subjects to claim themselves authorized by the said alleged communities or associations on pain of being considered instigators and protectors of illegal assemblies and associations and as such punishable according to the rigor of the regulations.

Article 4. Nor will those who consider themselves ministers or pastors of another religion than the Catholic religion be able to represent themselves as such in any act, wear in public any clothing different from that of others of the same religion, or appropriate for themselves any prerogative or distinction; we forbid them in particular from interfering in the issuance of certificates of marriage, birth or death, and we declare any such certificates to be from this moment null and void, without our judges or any others giving them consideration in any case whatsoever.

[Thirty-three other articles followed, most of them concerned with regulating the celebration of non-Catholic marriages.]

4

Letter from Rabaut Saint Etienne on the Edict of Toleration

December 6, 1787

A pastor from Nîmes, Jean Paul Rabaut Saint Etienne (1743–1793) often spoke for the Calvinist community. In this letter to an unidentified official in the government, he expresses some of the Calvinist reservations about the Edict of Toleration. He had closely followed its formulation

Bulletin de la Société de l'histoire du protestantisme français 33 (1884): 360–61, 363–64.

and knew the conflicts that lay behind the scenes of monarchical reform. In 1789, Rabaut Saint Etienne was elected as a deputy from the Third Estate of the Nîmes region, and he took an active part in the debates about the Declaration of the Rights of Man and Citizen. Like many of the most brilliant deputies of 1789, however, he fell victim to the increasingly radical revolutionary government that came into power after August 10, 1792. He was executed in Paris on December 5, 1793.[1]

Paris, December 6, 1787

Dear Sir,

I permit myself to do today what the public will do in a month's time [the edict was issued by the king in November 1787 but only officially registered by the Parlement in January 1788], that is, offer my observations on the famous edict that is going to occupy all of Europe and which, consequently, will be judged by it.

They have removed from the articles those which concerned public worship, but they have inserted at the end of the preamble the phrase *the Catholic religion will alone enjoy the RIGHTS and honors of public worship.* Since there is no mention in the edict of worship for non-Catholics, it is evident that the penal laws concerning the worship of Protestants remain intact, a situation that will not attract the favorable view of foreigners. And since this term *public worship* has whatever meaning one wants, when the law does not offer an interpretation it remains a vague expression, which leaves, in truth, all freedom of action to the government while at the same time maintaining the fears of both French nationals and foreigners. I make this observation, Sir, because it shows the necessity of quickly clarifying the status of worship, which cannot be public for Protestants, no doubt, but which must be *free.* Public worship for Protestants cannot be officially approved by a Catholic king but it must be unofficially tolerated by a king who is wise and politically astute.

They have moved into the preamble of the edict the thinking expressed by the Keeper of the Seals [a leading government official] in his speech on the subject: that non-Catholics *only get from the law what natural rights cannot refuse them, that is, the legal expression of their natural rights.* But we know today what natural rights are, and they certainly give to men much more than the edict accords to Protestants: it seems to me that it would have been better to suppress this thought. The time

---

[1] Information about the lives of deputies comes from Edna Hindie-Lemay, *Dictionnaire des Constituants, 1789–1791,* 2 vols. (Paris: Universitas, 1991).

has come when it is no longer acceptable for a law to overtly overrule the rights of humanity that are very well known all over the world.

Permit me, Sir, to complain as well about this vague expression of the preamble: *the non-Catholic subjects deprived of all influence on the established order in our state.* If this wording means that the Protestants will not participate in any kind of public administration, it says something that is not currently true, will not be true in the future, and cannot be possible. The legislator thereby opens the door to harassment of Protestants who, participating in various administrations, certainly have *influence*, albeit in small numbers, *on the established order in the state.* The legislator will close that door if he wants to confirm the current state of affairs and to establish what will be just and indispensable in the future. . . .

Article IV. They have suppressed (only recently) the phrase in this article that allowed Protestant ministers *to enjoy all civil rights like those of other non-Catholic subjects.*

This article was wise, it was just, it was politically astute: I dare say that its suppression is a defect.

It is only prudent to attach the ministers to the fatherland, and it can only be ill-advised to treat them like foreigners, for it cannot be wished that they be foreigners.

It is ill-advised to keep the penal laws, unless one wishes to retain the pleasure of enforcing them against Protestant ministers. By the now suppressed phrase, these were in effect abolished: by suppressing the phrase, one retains a shameful law, the opprobrium of a nation that claims and believes itself to be tolerant. . . .

I am insistent on this subject, Sir, as I was in the past, because I know public opinion. I hear everywhere the fears of the Protestant ministers that they are still forgotten and even proscribed. The little lambs of the flock are not themselves very reassured when one continues to oppress the shepherds, and they imagine that they too must suffer the same oppression and share it in some respects. I tried to reassure them in announcing the article that I have the honor of discussing with you, and I thought that this reassurance was necessary.

Even if they cannot see this at all, they can still perceive the emptiness of a law heralded long ago which limits itself to permitting Protestants to be goldsmiths or wigmakers and promises them that their children will no longer be bastards. This favor is no doubt great given the narrowness of minds in our country but it is not great in itself. It can only seem striking in a country where the law made concubines of wives for four generations [Calvinist marriages were not legally recognized after

1685] and where the principles of natural right are still so neglected that we are completely amazed by the tiny dwarf's steps taken in the reform of legislation.

They will be forced to attribute this reticence to something or to someone: and wherever their suspicion settles, neither advantage nor glory can come of it.

I therefore take the liberty, Sir, of imploring you to do whatever you can to reestablish this little phrase. I imagine that one has the intention of making Protestants a bit satisfied; for what is the good of a law if it proves to them that one has sought to assure the peace of mind of the ministers of government but not the peace of mind of the Protestant ministers. . . . I would not abuse your good will, Sir, if I was not entirely convinced that, without this article, one has accomplished almost nothing and that absolute silence on this matter will outrage the Catholics themselves and all of Europe. Thus, for the honor itself of the government, I will take care to say it again and again to the end of my strength; for, once the moment has passed, one would regret having refused such a simple request.

I beg your pardon, Sir, for the liberty that I continue to take until the moment when I will have nothing else to importune you with than the testimonials of an immortal recognition.

I am with profound respect, dear Sir, your humble and very obedient servant,
Rabaut Saint Etienne

5

ZALKIND HOURWITZ

Vindication of the Jews

1789

In 1789, forty thousand Jews lived in France, most of them in the eastern provinces of Alsace and Lorraine. In some respects, they were better treated than Calvinists under the laws of the monarchy; Jews could legally practice their religion, although their other activities were severely restricted. They had no civil or political rights, except the right to be judged by their own

Apologie des Juifs, en réponse à la question: Est-il des moyens de rendre les Juifs plus heureux et plus utiles en France? (Paris: Chez Gattey et chez Roger, 1789).

separate courts, and they faced pervasive local prejudice. The major Jewish communities—in the city of Bordeaux in the southwest and the regions of Alsace and Lorraine in the east—essentially constituted separate "nations" within the French nation (and nations separate from each other since their status differed in many ways).

In 1787 and 1788 the Royal Society of Arts and Sciences of the city of Metz in eastern France set up an essay competition on the question "Are there means for making the Jews happier and more useful in France?" Its two thousand Jews gave Metz the single largest Jewish population in the east. Among the three winners declared in 1788 was Zalkind Hourwitz (1738–1812), a Polish Jew. His pamphlet rapidly earned him a reputation in reformist circles, even though by today's standards its language seems moderate, if not excessively apologetic. The excerpt here represents what might be called the "assimilationist" position, that is, that granting rights to the Jews would make them more like the rest of the French. At times the author's own arguments sound anti-Semitic to our ears because in his concern to counter all the usual stereotypes about the Jews, he repeats many of them and gives them a kind of credit. As a follower of the Enlightenment, Zalkind Hourwitz disliked the extensive powers exercised by Jewish leaders over their communities, and he even held out the possibility of encouraging conversion to Christianity. The inclusion of such a suggestion and the defensive tone of the recommendations for improvement highlight the many difficulties and prejudices faced by the Jews.

The means of making the Jews happy and useful? Here it is: stop making them unhappy and unuseful. Accord them, or rather return to them the right of citizens, which you have denied them, against all divine and human laws and against your own interests, like a man who thoughtlessly cripples himself. . . .

To be sure, during times of barbarism, there was no shortage of ways of oppressing the Jews. Yet we are hard pressed even in an enlightened century, not to repair all the evils that have been done to them and to compensate them for their unjustly confiscated goods [hardly to be hoped for], but simply to cease being unjust toward them and to leave them peacefully to enjoy the rights of humanity under the protection of general laws. . . .

The simplest means would be therefore to accord them throughout the kingdom the same liberty that they enjoy in [Bordeaux and Bayonne]; nevertheless, however simple this means appears, it is still susceptible to greater perfection, in order to render the Jews not only happier and more useful but even more honest in the following manner.

1. They must be accorded permission to acquire land, which will attach them to the fatherland, where they will no longer regard themselves as foreigners and will increase at the same time the value of the land.

2. They must be permitted to practice all of the liberal and mechanical arts and agriculture, which will diminish the number of merchants among them and in consequence the number of knaves and rogues. . . .

4. To make their merchants more honest, they must be accorded the freedom to exercise every sort of commerce, to keep their stores open, to carry any product, and to live among the other citizens. Then being more closely allied with the other citizens, more at their ease and with their conduct more exposed to the inspection of the police, having moreover to manage their credit, their reputation and especially their regular customers, they will have in consequence less inclination, less necessity, and less facility in cheating and buying stolen goods.

5. To better diminish this facility in cheating, they must be forbidden, on pain of annulment of the transaction, the use of Hebrew and German [Yiddish] language and characters in their account books and commercial contracts, whether between themselves or with Christians.

6. It is necessary therefore to open the public schools to their children, to teach them French, which will produce a double advantage: it will make it easier to instruct them and to make them familiar from earliest infancy with Christians. They will establish with the Christians bonds of friendship which will be fortified by living near to each other, by the use of the same language and customs, and especially by the recognition of the freedom that they will be accorded; they will learn from these bonds that the Christians worship a Supreme Being like themselves, and as a result the fraud that the Talmud authorizes in dealings with pagans will no longer be permitted.

7. To better facilitate these bonds, their rabbis and leaders must be severely forbidden from claiming the least authority over their coreligionists outside of the synagogue, from prohibiting entry and honors to those who cut their beards, who curl their hair, who dress like Christians, who go to the theater, or who fail to observe some other custom that is irrelevant to their religion and only introduced by superstition in order to distinguish the Jews from other peoples. . . .

We could add that the freedom of the Jews is the best means of converting them to Christianity; for, once putting an end to their captivity,
you will render useless the temporal Messiah that they expect, and then
they will be obliged to recognize Jesus Christ as a spiritual Messiah in
order not to contradict the Prophets, who predicted the arrival of some
kind of Messiah. . . .

Are so many verbiages and citations necessary to prove that a Jew is
a man, and that it is unjust to punish him from his birth onward for real
or supposed vices that one reproaches in other men with whom he has
nothing in common but religious belief? And what would the French
say if the Academy of Stockholm had proposed, twelve years ago, the
following question: "Are there means for making Catholics more useful
and happier in Sweden?"

Antislavery Agitation

6

ABBÉ RAYNAL

From the *Philosophical and Political History of the Settlements and Trade of the Europeans in the East and West Indies*

1770

*Abbé Guillaume Thomas Raynal (1711–1796), known by his clerical
title [abbé = French for Father (a priest)], first published his multivolume history of European colonization anonymously in French in 1770.
Today many sections of it seem almost quaint and hopelessly detailed,
for Raynal and his collaborators (among them Diderot) gathered every*

*Philosophical and Political History of the Settlements and Trade of the Europeans in the
East and West Indies,* revised, augmented, and published, 10 vols., by Abbé Raynal.
Newly translated from the French, by J. O. Justamond, F.R.S., 8 vols. (London: W. Stra-
han, 1783). Excerpted from vol. 5, bk. XI: 292–96, 302–4, 307–10. This edition appears
to be a translation of the 1780 Geneva edition in French, whose passages on slavery
sounded a more combative note than those found in the original 1770 edition.

imaginable fact to support their scathing indictment of European rapaciousness. As the English man of letters and diarist Horace Walpole commented, "It tells one everything in the world," from the story of the tea and coffee trades to naval battles to the history of Greek and Roman slavery.[1] In its time, the book startled and shocked, and its indignant denunciation of colonization set off a firestorm of controversy. The French Crown immediately prohibited its sale on the grounds that it contained "propositions that are impudent, dangerous, rash and contrary to good morals and the principles of religion."

The government forced Raynal into exile, and an assembly of the French clergy condemned him as "one of the most seditious writers among modern unbelievers."[2] Thanks to its notoriety, the book soon became a bestseller appearing in multiple editions, approved and pirated, in French, English, and Spanish. Slaveowners must have shuddered, however, when they read the passages that follow, for in them the slave trade and the practice of slavery are condemned and a future uprising of the slaves against their masters is predicted.

Liberty is the property of one's self. Three kinds of it are distinguished. Natural liberty, civil liberty, and political liberty: that is to say, the liberty of the individual, the liberty of the citizen, and the liberty of a nation. Natural liberty is the right granted by nature to every man to dispose of himself at pleasure. Civil liberty is the right which is insured by society to every citizen, of doing every thing which is not contrary to the laws. Political liberty is the state of a people who have not alienated their sovereignty, and who either make their own law, or who constitute a part in the system of their legislation.

The first of these liberties is, after reason, the distinguishing characteristic of man. Brutes are chained up, and kept in subjection, because they have no notion of what is just or unjust, no idea of grandeur or meanness. But in man, liberty is the principle of his vices or his virtues. None but a free man can say, *I will*, or *I will not*; and consequently none but a free man can be worthy of praise, or be liable to censure.

Without liberty, or the property of one's own body, and the enjoyment of one's mind, no man can be either a husband, a father, a relation, or a

---

[1] Carl Ludwig Lokke, *France and the Colonial Question: A Study of Contemporary French Opinion, 1763–1801* (1932; reprint, New York: AMS Press, 1968), 48.

[2] As quoted in Anatole Feugère, *L'Abbé Raynal (1713–1796): Un précurseur de la Révolution* (1922; reprint, Geneva: Slatkine Reprints, 1970), 267, 271.

friend; he hath neither country, a fellow citizen, nor a God. The slave, impelled by the wicked man, and who is the instrument of his wickedness, is inferior even to the dog, let loose by the Spaniard upon the American; for conscience, which the dog has not, still remains with the man. He who basely abdicates his liberty, gives himself up to remorse, and to the greatest misery which can be experienced by a thinking and sensible being. If there be not any power under the heavens, which can change my nature and reduce me to the state of brutes, there is none which can dispose of my liberty. God is my father, and not my master; I am his child, and not his slave. How is it possible that I should grant to political power, what I refuse to divine omnipotence?

Will these eternal and immutable truths, the foundation of all morality, the basis of all rational government, be contested? They will, and the audacious argument will be dictated by barbarous and sordid avarice. Behold that proprietor of a vessel, who leaning upon his desk, and with the pen in his hand, regulates the number of enormities he may cause to be committed on the Coasts of Guinea; who considers at leisure, what number of firelocks [guns] he shall want to obtain one Negro, what fetters will be necessary to keep him chained on board his ship, what whips will be required to make him work; who calculates with coolness, every drop of blood which the slave must necessarily expend in labour for him, and how much it will produce; who considers whether a Negro woman will be of more advantage to him by her feeble labours, or by going through the dangers of childbirth. You shudder!—If there existed any religion which tolerated, or which gave only a tacit sanction to such kind of horrors; if, absorbed in some idle or seditious questions, it did not incessantly exclaim against the authors or the instruments of this tyranny; if it should consider it as a crime in a slave to break his chains; if it should suffer to remain in it's [sic] community, the iniquitous judge who condemns the fugitive to death: if such a religion, I say, existed, ought not the minister of it to be suffocated under the ruins of their altars? . . .

But, it is alleged, that in all regions, and in all ages, slavery hath been more or less established.

I grant it; but what doth it signify to me, what other people in other ages have done? Are we to appeal to the customs of antient [sic] times, or to our conscience? Are we to listen to the suggestions of interest, of infatuation, and of barbarism, rather than to those of reason and of justice? If the universality of a practice were admitted as a proof of it's [sic] innocence, we should then have a complete apology for usurpations, conquests, and for every species of oppression. [The author then refutes other reasons given in support of slavery.] . . .

But it is urged, that in Europe, as well as in America, the people are slaves. The only advantage we have over the Negroes is, that we can break one chain to put on another.

It is but too true; most nations are enslaved. The multitude is generally sacrificed to the passions of a few privileged oppressors. There is scarce a region know'n, where a man can flatter himself that he is master of his person, that he can dispose, at pleasure, of his inheritance; and that he can quietly enjoy the fruits of his industry. Even in those countries that are least under the yoke of servitude, the citizen deprived of the produce of his labour, by the wants incessantly renewed of a rapacious or needy government, is continually restrained in the most lawful means of acquiring felicity. Liberty is stifled in all parts, by extravagant superstitions, by barbarous customs, and by obsolete laws. It will one day certainly rise again from it's [*sic*] ashes. In proportion as morality and policy shall be improved, man will recover his rights. But wherefore, while we are waiting for these fortunate times, and these enlightened ages of prosperity wherefore must there be an unfortunate race, to whom even the comfortable and honourable name of freeman is denied, and who, notwithstanding the instability of events, must be deprived of the hope even of obtaining it? Whatever, therefore, may be said, the condition of these unfortunate people is very different from our's [*sic*]. . . .

I have already said too much for the honest and feeling man. I shall never be able to say enough for the inhuman trader.

Let us, therefore, hasten to substitute the light of reason and the sentiments of nature to the blind ferociousness of our ancestors. Let us break the bonds of so many victims to our mercenary principles, should we even be obliged to discard a commerce which is founded only on injustice, and the object of which is luxury. . . .

[The author then proposes that those currently living as slaves should continue in that status; only their children would be freed after the age of twenty.]

While we are restoring these unhappy beings to liberty, we must be careful to subject them to our laws and manners, and to offer them our superfluities. We must give them a country, give them interests to study, productions to cultivate, and articles of consumption agreeable to their respective tastes, and our colonies will never want hands, which being eased of their chains, will become more active and robust. . . .

[The author calls on the monarchs of Europe to abolish the slave trade, but he concludes with a warning of impending slave revolt.]

Let the ineffectual calls of humanity be no longer pleaded with the people and their masters: perhaps, they have never been attended to in any public transactions. If then, ye nations of Europe, interest alone can exert it's [sic] influence over you, listen to me once more. Your slaves stand in no need either of your generosity or your counsels, in order to break the sacrilegious yoke of their oppression. Nature speaks a more powerful language than philosophy, or interests. Already have two colonies of fugitive Negroes been established, to whom treaties and power give a perfect security from your attempts.[3] These are so many indications of the impending storm, and the Negroes only want a chief, sufficiently courageous, to lead them on to vengeance and slaughter.

Where is this great man, whom nature owes to her afflicted, oppressed, and tormented children? Where is he? He will undoubtedly appear, he will shew himself, he will lift up the sacred standard of liberty. This venerable signal will collect around him the companions of his misfortunes. They will rush on with more impetuosity than torrents; they will leave behind them, in all parts, indelible traces of their just resentment. Spaniards, Portugueze [sic], English, French, Dutch, all their tyrants will become the victims of fire and sword. The plains of America will suck up with transport the blood which they have so long expected, and the bones of so many wretches, heaped upon one another, during the course of so many centuries, will bound for joy. The Old World will join it's [sic] plaudits to those of the New. In all parts the name of the hero, who shall have restored the rights of the human species will be blest; in all parts trophies will be erected to his glory. Then will the *black code* [each country had its own code of laws regarding slaves or blacks] be no more; and the *white code* will be a dreadful one, if the conqueror only regards the right of reprisals.

---

[3]The author has in mind the fugitive slaves in Jamaica and Dutch Surinam, but almost every colony in the Americas with slaves had its runaway slave societies. The largest ones could be found in the Caribbean and in the interior of the eastern South American coast.

7

CONDORCET

Reflections on Negro Slavery

1781

By the 1780s the European slave trade had become a very contentious issue. Even the ministers of the French monarchy began to feel at least private doubts about the morality of enslaving Africans. There were as yet, however, few public calls for abolition. In 1781 one of the leading French reformers, the nobleman Marie Jean Caritat, Marquis de Condorcet (1743–1794), published under a pseudonym an impassioned pamphlet against slavery. In it he denounced the slave system as a crime and called for its abolition without compensation. He associated these demands with other calls for reform, including restoration of the civil rights of Calvinists, the elimination of torture in the judicial process, and the suppression of the last remains of serfdom. In 1788, Condorcet helped found the Society of the Friends of Blacks, which imported English and American abolitionist ideas into France. One of the most consistent and outspoken defenders of human rights, Condorcet also publicly supported the rights of women during the Revolution. His renown did not save him, however, from the internal political struggles that divided the political factions within the new republic. He killed himself in 1794 while in prison awaiting execution for opposing the policies of the increasingly radical revolutionary government. On the question of rights, Condorcet was more thoroughgoing in his approach than anyone else. On other issues, he disagreed with those leading the emergency government of the new republic. The same leaders who ordered his arrest and execution also urged the suppression of women's political clubs.

"Dedicatory Epistle to the Negro Slaves"

My Friends,

Although I am not the same color as you, I have always regarded you as my brothers. Nature formed you with the same spirit, the same

Oeuvres complètes de Condorcet, ed. D. J. Garat and P. J. G. Cabanis, 21 vols. (Paris: Ch. Fr. Cramer, 1802), 11:85, 88, 93, 124–25, 191–94.

reason, the same virtues as whites. . . . Your tyrants will reproach me with uttering only commonplaces and having nothing but chimerical ideas: indeed, nothing is more common than the maxims of humanity and justice; nothing is more chimerical than to propose to men that they base their conduct on them.

REFLECTIONS ON NEGRO SLAVERY

Reducing a man to slavery, buying him, selling him, keeping him in servitude: these are truly crimes, and crimes worse than theft. In effect, they take from the slave, not only all forms of property but also the ability to acquire it, the control over his time, his strength, of everything that nature has given him to maintain his life and satisfy his needs. To this wrong they add that of taking from the slave the right to dispose of his own person. . . .

It follows from our principles that the inflexible justice to which kings and nations are subject like their citizens requires the destruction of slavery. We have shown that this destruction will harm neither commerce nor the wealth of a nation because it would not result in any decrease in cultivation. We have shown that the master had no right over his slave; that the act of keeping him in servitude is not the enjoyment of a property right but a crime; that in freeing the slave the law does not attack property but rather ceases to tolerate an action which it should have punished with the death penalty. The sovereign therefore owes no compensation to the master of slaves just as he owes none to a thief whom a court judgment has deprived of the possession of a stolen good. The public tolerance of a crime may make punishment impossible but it cannot grant a real right to the profit from the crime. . . .

The protection accorded to rapacity against the Negroes, which in England and Holland is the effect of the general corruption of these nations, has for its cause in Spain and in France only the prejudices of the public and the taking unawares of governments that are deceived equally about both the necessity of slavery and the supposed political importance of the sugar colonies [in the Caribbean]. A foreigner's writing can be especially useful in France, for it will not be so easy to destroy the effect of a single word by saying that it is the work of a *philosophe* [supporter of Enlightenment reform].[1] This name, so respectable elsewhere,

---

[1]*Philosophe* in French means philosopher, but in the eighteenth century it became the shorthand term for a supporter of the Enlightenment, someone who believed that reason could be used to criticize current practices and point the way to much-needed reforms in all areas of social life. Here Condorcet shows how loaded the term had become.

has become an insult in this nation. . . . If writers protest against the slavery of Negroes, it is the *philosophes*, their opponents say, thinking they have won their case. . . . If some people have been saved by innoculation from the dangers of smallpox, it's by the advice of the *philosophes*. . . . If the custom of breaking the bones of the accused between boards to make them tell the truth has been recently suppressed, it's because the *philosophes* inveighed against the practice; and it is in spite of the *philosophes* that France has been lucky enough to save a remnant of the old laws and conserve the precious practice of applying torture to condemned criminals. . . . Who is it who dares to complain in France about the barbarism of the criminal laws, about the cruelty with which the French Protestants have been deprived of the rights of man and citizen, about the harshness and injustice of the laws against smuggling and on hunting? Who had the culpable boldness to pretend that it would be useful to the people and in accord with justice to insure liberty of commerce and industry? . . . We can see clearly that it was surely the *philosophes*.

8

SOCIETY OF THE FRIENDS OF BLACKS

Discourse on the Necessity of Establishing in Paris a Society for . . . the Abolition of the Slave Trade and of Negro Slavery

1788

Following the lead of English and American abolitionists, French reformers, among them Condorcet, founded the Society of the Friends of Blacks in February 1788 to agitate for the abolition of the slave trade and of slavery. The speech given by Jacques Brissot to announce its foundation

Discours sur la nécéssité d'établir à Paris une Société pour concourir, avec celle de Londres, à l'abolition de la traite et de l'esclavage des Nègres. Prononcé le 19 février 1788, dans une Société de quelques amis, rassemblés à Paris, à la prière du Comité de Londres (Paris, 1788), 6–7, 9, 31–32. This pamphlet was published anonymously, but it has been attributed to Brissot.

*shows the influence of the Enlightenment rhetoric of liberty and reason,
and it appears to endorse, although without much fanfare, the notion
of universal, equal human rights. Most in the society stopped short of
advocating the outright and immediate abolition of slavery itself however,
and instead argued for a gradual process of emancipation. The society
obviously did not expect immediate success, for it couched its demands in
vague terms, hoping for a positive response from a reform-minded monarchy that had recently acted in favor of the Calvinists.*

In a free society, man is drawn by his personal interest to develop his
faculties to the highest degree. In a free society, one can only be governed by universal reason, and universal reason essentially compels us
to want peace and the good of all men. In committing myself to these
agreeable ideas, I cannot stop myself, good sirs, from remarking on the
error of those who wish to enlighten men living in servitude but without destroying it. You hear shouted everywhere, "enlighten men and
they will become better"; but the experience of all the centuries tells us,
"make men free, and they will necessarily and rapidly become enlightened, and they will necessarily be better." . . .

Thus, if we seriously wish to enlighten men and improve their social
and individual state, we should not limit ourselves to giving them books
or academies; we should untie their hands. . . . How, in fact, can a man
value books when he sees men who preach such values violate the first
of truths: *all men are born free?* Must he not believe then that he is being
manipulated by the vilest hypocrisy? . . .

Freedom—Upon returning it to the Negroes, stop then fearing
them: having become our brothers, they will not wait to enlighten themselves, to become good, and what is perhaps more difficult, the Masters
themselves will be forced to become enlightened, to become good; for
slavery is an infallible means of corrupting two men at the same time,
the Master and the Slave. . . .

Let us remember the character of our Nation, a character more than
any other imprinted with universal benevolence. Let us remember finally
the wishes of the present Ministry for the eradication of every kind of
abuse and its readiness to receive ideas for reform. When it sees the
Nation convinced that the slavery of Negroes is a crime, and that nature
wisely attached more real advantages to the labor of liberty than to that
of servitude, will the Ministry lean toward itself presenting to the Sovereign a universal desire that its heart must receive with eagerness? Its
predecessors solemnly declared, *that all men were free by Nature; that the*

Kingdom of the Franks must be free in reality as well as in name. Guided by this principle, they have one after another emancipated the serfs of their lands. Our Monarch has himself abolished the last remains of that servitude.[1] How could his benevolent hand not be extended one day toward the Negroes who live under his Laws? Are not the French Colonies part of his Lands? Are not the Negroes his subjects, just like the Whites who inhabit them?

[1] In 1778, Louis XVI abolished the last traces of serfdom on all royal lands. The last French serfs in private hands got their freedom from the National Assembly in 1789.

Women Begin to Agitate for Rights

9

"Petition of Women of the Third Estate to the King"
January 1, 1789

Little is known about women's grievances or feelings in the months leading up to the meeting of the Estates General. They did not have the right to meet as a group, draft grievances, or vote (except in isolated individual instances) in the preparatory elections. Nevertheless, some women did put their thoughts to paper, and although little evidence exists about the circumstances or the identities of those involved, the few documents offering their views bear witness to their concerns in this time of ferment. In this document working women addressed the king in respectful terms and carefully insisted that they did not wish to overturn men's authority; they simply wanted the education and enlightenment that would make them better workers, better wives, and better mothers. The petitioners expressed their deep apprehensions about prostitutes and the fear that they would be confused with them; like prostitutes, working women did not stay at home but necessarily entered the public sphere to make their livings. Most of all, however, the women wanted to be heard; they saw the opening created

---

Pétition des femmes du tiers-état au Roi (n.p., but almost certainly Paris, January 1, 1789 — this is probably not the actual date of publication but a signal that the writers hoped that 1789 would inaugurate a new state of affairs for women, too).

by the convocation of the Estates General and hoped to make their own claims for inclusion in the promised reforms.

Sire,
At a time when the different orders of the state are occupied with their interests; when everyone seeks to make the most of his titles and rights; when some anxiously recall the centuries of servitude and anarchy, while others make every effort to shake off the last links that still bind them to the imperious remains of feudalism; women—continual objects of the admiration and scorn of men—could they not also make their voices heard midst this general agitation?

Excluded from the national assemblies by laws so well consolidated that they allow no hope of infringement, they do not ask, Sire, for your permission to send their deputies to the Estates General; they know too well how much favor will play a part in the election, and how easy it would be for those elected to impede the freedom of voting.

We prefer, Sire, to place our cause at your feet; not wishing to obtain anything except from your heart, it is to it that we address our complaints and confide our miseries.

The women of the Third Estate are almost all born without wealth; their education is very neglected or very defective: it consists in their being sent to school with a teacher who himself does not know the first word of the language [Latin] he teaches. They continue to go there until they can read the service of the Mass in French and Vespers in Latin. Having fulfilled the first duties of religion, they are taught to work; having reached the age of fifteen or sixteen, they can earn five or six *sous* a day. If nature has refused them beauty they get married, without a dowry, to unfortunate artisans; lead aimless, difficult lives stuck in the provinces; and give birth to children they are incapable of raising. If, on the contrary, they are born pretty, without breeding, without principles, with no idea of morals, they become the prey of the first seducer, commit a first sin, come to Paris to bury their shame, end by losing it altogether, and die victims of dissolute ways.

Today, when the difficulty of subsisting forces thousands of them to put themselves up for auction [prostitution], when men find it easier to buy them for a short time than to win them over forever, those whom a fortunate penchant inclines to virtue, who are consumed by the desire to learn, who feel themselves carried along by a natural taste, who have overcome the deficiencies of their education and know a little of everything without having learned anything, those, finally, whom a lofty soul, a noble heart, and a pride of sentiment cause to be called *prudes*, are obliged to throw themselves into cloisters where only a modest dowry is required, or forced to become servants if they do not have enough courage, enough heroism, to share the generous devotion of the girls of Vincent de Paul.[1]

Also, many, solely because they are born girls, are disdained by their parents, who refuse to set them up, preferring to concentrate their fortune in the hands of a son whom they designate to carry on their name in the capital; for Your Majesty should know that we too have names to keep up. Or, if old age finds them spinsters, they spend it in tears and see themselves the object of the scorn of their nearest relatives.

To prevent so many ills, Sire, we ask that men not be allowed, under any pretext, to exercise trades that are the prerogative of women — whether as seamstress, embroiderer, millinery shopkeeper, etc., etc.; if we are left at least with the needle and the spindle, we promise never to handle the compass or the square.

We ask, Sire, that your benevolence provide us with the means of making the most of the talents with which nature will have endowed us, notwithstanding the impediments which are forever being placed on our education.

May you assign us positions, which we alone will be able to fill, which we will occupy only after having passed a strict examination, following trustworthy inquiries concerning the purity of our morals.

We ask to be enlightened, to have work, not in order to usurp men's authority, but in order to be better esteemed by them, so that we might have the means of living safe from misfortune and so that poverty does not force the weakest among us, who are blinded by luxury and swept along by example, to join the crowd of unfortunate women who overpopulate the streets and whose *debauched* audacity disgraces our sex and the men who keep them company.

We would wish this class of women might wear a mark of identification. Today, when they adopt even the modesty of our dress, when they mingle everywhere in all kinds of clothing, we often find ourselves confused with them; some men make mistakes and make us blush because of their scorn. They should never be able to take off the identification under pain of working in public workshops for the benefit of the poor (it is known that work is the greatest punishment that can be inflicted on them). . . . However, it occurs to us that the empire of fashion would be destroyed and one would run the risk of seeing many too many women dressed in the same color.

---

[1]Saint Vincent de Paul organized communities for women who served as schoolteachers, nurses, and the like. They took simple vows, did not wear religious costumes, and worked outside in the community rather than staying in their convent. These communities often appealed to poor women but demanded hard work.

We implore you, Sire, to set up free schools where we might learn our language on the basis of principles, religion and ethics. May one and the other be offered to us in all their grandeur, entirely stripped of the petty applications which attenuate their majesty; may our hearts be formed there; may we be taught above all to practice the virtues of our sex: gentleness, modesty, patience, charity. As for the arts that please, women learn them without teachers. Sciences? . . . they serve only to inspire us with a stupid pride, lead us to pedantry, go against the wishes of nature, make of us mixed beings who are rarely faithful wives and still more rarely good mothers of families.

We ask to take leave of ignorance, to give our children a sound and reasonable education so as to make of them subjects worthy of serving you. We will teach them to cherish the beautiful name of Frenchmen; we will transmit to them the love we have for Your Majesty. For we are certainly willing to leave valor and genius to men, but we will always challenge them over the dangerous and precious gift of sensibility; we defy them to love you better than we do. They run to Versailles, most of them for their interests, while we, Sire, go to see you there, and when with difficulty and with pounding hearts, we can gaze for an instance upon your August Person, tears flow from our eyes. The idea of Majesty, of the Sovereign, vanishes, and we see in you only a tender Father, for whom we would give our lives a thousand times.

Categories of Citizenship

10

ABBÉ SIEYÈS

What Is the Third Estate?

January 1789

In his book-sized pamphlet, Abbé Emmanuel Joseph Sieyès (1748–1836) turned the usual discussion about voting procedures in the forthcoming Estates General into a searing critique of French political and social

Abbé Sieyès, *Qu'est-ce que le tiers état?* (Paris, 1789). This first edition of the work was published in early January 1789.

inequities and in particular the privileges of the nobility. At issue were not the rights of small minorities or enslaved peoples far away in colonies, but rather the most fundamental features of the French social order at home. He dropped the common polite and even apologetic tone taken by most non-noble commentators and forcefully pronounced the right of the Third Estate to be "everything." Sieyès went on to become one of the most influential theorists of the French Revolution, although hardly its most radical one. In 1799 he helped bring Napoleon Bonaparte to power, thus ending the revolutionary experiment in favor of a more authoritarian solution.

The plan of this work is quite simple. We must ask ourselves three questions.

1. What is the Third Estate? Everything.

2. What has it been until now in the political order? Nothing.

3. What does it want? To become something. . . .

What does a Nation require to survive and prosper? *Private* employment and *public* offices.

Private employment includes four classes of work:

1. Since the land and water provide the raw material for the needs of mankind, the first class, in logical order, includes all those families attached to work in the countryside.

2. Between the initial sale of raw materials and their consumption or usage as finished goods, labor of various sorts adds more value to these goods. In this way human industry manages to improve on the blessings of Nature and to multiply the value of the raw materials two, ten, or a hundredfold. Such is the second class of work.

3. Between production and consumption, as also between the different stages of production, there are a host of intermediary agents, useful both to producers and consumers; these are the merchants and wholesale traders. Wholesale traders constantly weigh demand according to place and time and speculate on the profit that they can make on storage and transport; merchants actually sell the goods on the markets, whether wholesale or retail. This type of utility designates the third class of work.

4. Besides these three classes of hard-working and useful Citizens who occupy themselves with the *things* fit to be consumed or

used, society also needs a multitude of private occupations and services *directly* useful or agreeable to the *person*. This fourth class embraces all those occupations from the most distinguished scientific and liberal professions down to the least esteemed domestic services.

These are the kinds of work that sustain society. Who carries them out? The Third Estate.

In the present state of affairs public offices can also be ranked in four well-known categories: the Sword [the army], the Robe [the courts], the Church, and the Administration. Detailed analysis is not necessary to show that the Third Estate makes up everywhere 19/20ths of their number, except that it is charged with all the really hard work, all the work that the privileged order refuses to perform. Only the lucrative and most honored places are taken by the members of the privileged order. Should we praise them for this? We could do so only if the Third [Estate] was unwilling or unable to fill these offices. We know the truth of the matter, but the Third Estate has nonetheless been excluded. They are told, "Whatever your services, whatever your talents, you will only go so far and no further. Honors are not for your sort." A few rare exceptions, noteworthy as they are bound to be, are only a mockery, and the language encouraged on these exceptional occasions is but an additional insult.

If this exclusion is a social crime committed against the Third Estate, can we say at least that it is useful to the public good? Ah! Are the effects of monopoly not known? If it discourages those whom it pushes aside, does it not also render those it favors less competent? Is it not obvious that every piece of work kept out of free competition will be made more expensively and less well?

When any office is deemed the prerogative of a separate order among the citizens, has no one noticed that a salary has to be paid not only to the man who does the work but also to all those of the same caste who do not and even to entire families of both those who work and those who do not? Has no one noticed that this state of affairs, so abjectly respected among us, nonetheless seems contemptible and shameful in the history of ancient Egypt and in the stories of voyages to the Indies? But let us leave aside those considerations which though broadening our purview and perhaps enlightening would only slow our pace. It suffices here to have made the point that the supposed usefulness of a privileged order to the public service is nothing but a mirage; that without that order, all that is most arduous in this service is performed by the Third Estate; that without the privileged the best places would be infinitely better filled; that such places should naturally be the prize and reward for recognized talents and services; and that if the privileged have succeeded in usurping all the lucrative and honored posts, this is at once an odious iniquity committed against the vast majority of the citizenry and an act of treason against the public good.

Who therefore dares to say that the Third Estate does not contain within itself all that is needed to form a complete Nation? The Third Estate is like a strong and robust man with one arm still in chains. If we remove the privileged order, the Nation will not be something less but something more. Thus, what is the Third Estate? All, but an all that is shackled and oppressed. What would it be without the privileged order? All, but an all that is free and flourishing. Nothing can be done without it [the Third Estate]; everything would be infinitely better without the other two orders.

It does not suffice to have demonstrated that the privileged, far from being useful to the Nation, can only weaken and harm it; it must be proved further that the noble order[1] is not even part of society itself: It may very well be a burden for the Nation but it cannot be a part of it.

First, it is not possible to assign a place to the caste of nobles among the many elements that make up a Nation. I know that there are too many individuals whose infirmities, incapacity, incurable laziness, or excessively bad morals make them essentially foreigners to the work of society. The exception and the abuse always accompany the rule, especially in a vast empire. But at least we can agree that the fewer the abuses, the better ordered the state. The worst-off state of all would be the one in which not only isolated individual cases but also an entire class of citizens would glory in inactivity amidst the general movement and would contrive to consume the best part of what is produced without having contributed anything to its making. Such a class is surely foreign to the Nation because of its *idleness.*

---

[1] [Sieyès's own note] I do not speak of the clergy here. In my way of thinking, the clergy is not an order but rather a profession charged with a public service. In the clergy, it is not the person who is privileged but the office, which is very different. . . . The word caste refers to a class of men who, without functions and without usefulness and by the sole fact that they exist, enjoy the privileges attached to their person. From this point of view, which is the true one in my opinion, there is only one order, that of the nobility. They are truly a people apart but a false people, which not being able to exist by itself by reason of its lack of useful organs, attaches itself to a real Nation like those plant growths which can only survive on the sap of the plants that they tire and suck dry. The Clergy, the Robe, the Sword, and the Administration are four classes of public trustees that are necessary everywhere. Why are they accused in France of *aristocraticism?* It is because the noble caste has usurped all the good positions; it has done so as if this was a patrimonial property exploited for its personal profit rather than in the spirit of social welfare.

The noble order is no less foreign amongst us by reason of its *civil* and *public* prerogatives.

What is a Nation? A body of associates living under a *common* law and represented by the same *legislature.*

Is it not more than certain that the noble order has privileges, exemptions, and even rights that are distinct from the rights of the great body of citizens? Because of this, it does not belong to the common order, it is not covered by the law common to the rest. Thus its civil rights already make it a people apart inside the great Nation. It is truly *imperium in imperio* [a law unto itself].

As for its *political* rights, the nobility also exercises them separately. It has its own representatives who have no mandate from the people. Its deputies sit separately, and even when they assemble in the same room with the deputies of the ordinary citizens, the nobility's representation still remains essentially distinct and separate: it is foreign to the Nation by its very principle, for its mission does not emanate from the people, and by its purpose, since it consists in defending, not the general interest, but the private interests of the nobility.

The Third Estate therefore contains everything that pertains to the Nation and nobody outside of the Third Estate can claim to be part of the Nation. What is the Third Estate? EVERYTHING. . . .

By Third Estate is meant the collectivity of citizens who belong to the common order. Anybody who holds a legal privilege of any kind leaves that common order, stands as an exception to the common law, and in consequence does not belong to the Third Estate. . . . It is certain that the moment a citizen acquires privileges contrary to common law, he no longer belongs to the common order. His new interest is opposed to the general interest; he has no right to vote in the name of the people. [Thus nobles should not be allowed to represent the Third Estate in the Estates General.] . . .

[In the process of arguing against the possibility of nobles being chosen to represent the Third Estate, Sieyès stated some of the commonly held assumptions about the right to vote.]

In no circumstances can any freedom or right be without limitations. In every country, the law has prescribed certain qualifications without which one can be neither a voter nor eligible for office. Thus, for example, the law must set an age below which one would not qualify to represent his fellow citizens. Similarly, women are everywhere, rightly or wrongly, excluded from exercising these kinds of mandates. It goes without saying that a vagrant or beggar cannot be charged with the political confidence of their countrymen. Would a servant or anyone dependent on a master, or a non-naturalized foreigner, be allowed to take places among the representatives of a Nation? Political liberty therefore has its limits just like civil liberty. . . .

In vain can anyone's eyes be closed to the revolution that time and the force of things have brought to pass; it is none the less real. Once upon a time the Third Estate was in bondage and the noble order was everything that mattered. Today the Third is everything and nobility but a word. Yet under the cover of this word a new and intolerable aristocracy has slipped in, and the people has every reason to no longer want aristocrats. . . .

What is the will of a Nation? It is the result of individual wills, just as the Nation is the aggregate of the individuals who compose it. It is impossible to conceive of a legitimate association that does not have for its goal the common security, the common liberty, in short, the public good. No doubt each individual also has his own personal aims. He says to himself, "protected by the common security, I will be able to peacefully pursue my own personal projects, I will seek my happiness where I will, assured of encountering only those legal obstacles that society will prescribe for the common interest, in which I have a part and with which my own personal interest is so usefully allied." . . .

Three kinds of interests can be found in the hearts of men: 1) that which makes them all alike; it marks the boundaries of the common interest, 2) that which unites an individual to only some others; this is the interest of a body or group; and finally, 3) that which isolates each person and makes him think only of himself; this is a personal interest. The interest whereby a man comes to an agreement with all of his associates is obviously the purpose toward which everyone's will and that of the common assembly both tend. The influence of personal interest ought to count for nothing in this domain. That is in fact what happens, for the diversity of interest is its own remedy. The great difficulty comes from that interest whereby a citizen agrees with only some others. This permits them to connive and conspire to devise schemes that are dangerous for the community interest; this kind of interest creates the most formidable enemies of the people. History presents countless examples of this truth.

It is therefore not surprising that social order rigorously demands that ordinary citizens refrain from constituting themselves in *corporations* [such as guilds]; it even requires that public officials, who of necessity form true *corps* or official bodies, renounce the possibility of being elected to the legislature as long as they are so employed.

Thus and not otherwise is the common interest assured of dominating over personal interests. Only under these conditions can one accept the possibility of founding human associations for the general advantage of those so associated and as a result grant the *legitimacy* of political societies or clubs. . . .

Advantages which differentiate citizens from one another lie outside the purview of citizenship. Inequalities of wealth or ability are like the inequalities of age, sex, size, etc. In no way do they detract from the *equality* of citizenship. These individual advantages no doubt benefit from the protection of the law; but it is not the legislator's task to create them, to give privileges to some and refuse them to others. The law grants nothing; it protects what already exists until such time that what exists begins to harm the common interest. These are the only limits on individual freedom. I imagine the law as being at the center of a large globe; we the citizens, without exception, stand equidistant from it on the surface and occupy equal places; all are equally dependent on the law, all present it with their liberty and their property to be protected; and this is what I call the *common rights* of citizens, by which they are all alike. All these individuals communicate with each other, enter into contracts, negotiate, always under the common guarantee of the law. If in this general activity somebody wishes to get control over the person of his neighbor or usurp his property, the common law goes into action to repress this criminal attempt and puts everyone back in their place at the same distance from the law. . . .

It is impossible to say what place the two privileged orders ought to occupy in the social order: this is the equivalent of asking what place one wishes to assign to a malignant tumor that torments and undermines the strength of the body of a sick person. It must be *neutralized.* We must re-establish the health and working of all the organs so thoroughly that they are no longer susceptible to these fatal schemes that are capable of sapping the most essential principles of vitality.

2

The Declaration of the Rights of Man and Citizen, 1789

Debates about the Declaration of Rights, July and August 1789

Even before the fall of the Bastille on July 14, 1789, the deputies in the new National Assembly had begun to debate the preparation of a declaration of rights. Many considered such a declaration a necessary preliminary to any constitution. Others resisted the idea of a declaration as dangerous because it would raise popular expectations of massive changes. The debates offer a panorama of contemporary perceptions of the significance of human rights and the necessity or not of proclaiming them.

11

MARQUIS DE LAFAYETTE

July 11, 1789

Marie Joseph du Motier, Marquis de Lafayette (1757–1834), enjoyed unparalleled prestige at the beginning of the French Revolution. Having gained a heroic reputation for his participation in the War of American Independence on the side of the colonists, he only increased his stature when he argued vociferously for reform in France from as early as 1787. As a deputy from the nobility to the Estates General, he established

---

Archives parlementaires de 1787 à 1860: Recueil complet des débats législatifs et politiques des chambres françaises, Series 1 (hereafter *Archives parlementaires*), 8 (Paris, 1875): 221–22, 320, 322–23.

himself as a leader of the liberal nobles who took the side of the Third Estate. His election as commander of the new Parisian National Guard took him away from most of the debates in the National Assembly, but his intervention on July 11 opened the discussion and provided the first model for the future declaration. Lafayette's proposed declaration had been drawn up with the advice of Thomas Jefferson.

In effect, whether you would immediately offer to the nation this enunciation of incontestable truths or would think that this first chapter of your great work should not be set apart from it [the constitution], it is established that your ideas must at once fix on a declaration that contains the first principles of any constitution, the first elements of all legislation. However simple, however common even are these principles, it will often prove useful to bring the discussions of the Assembly back to them.

[In these early days of the National Assembly, the newspapers sometimes reported speeches word for word and sometimes summarized them. The next segment is a summary.] Monsieur de Lafayette next presented two reasons for the utility of a declaration of rights. [It then returns to a word-for-word rendition.]

The first [reason for a declaration] is to recall the sentiments that nature has engraved on the heart of every individual and to facilitate the development of them, which is all the more interesting in that, for a nation to love liberty, it suffices that it be acquainted with it, and for it to be free, it suffices that it wishes it.

The second reason is to express these eternal truths from which all institutions should be derived and to become, in the labors of the representatives of the nation, a loyal guide that always leads them back to the source of natural and social right. . . .

The merit of a declaration of rights consists in truth and precision; it should say what everyone knows, what everyone feels. It is only this idea, Sirs, that could have engaged me to offer the draft that I have the honor of presenting to you.

Far be it from me to ask that it be adopted; I ask only that the Assembly have copies made to be distributed in the different sub-committees; this first effort on my part will push other members to present other projects which will better fulfill the wishes of the Assembly, and which I will eagerly prefer to my own.

[Then follows his project, much briefer than the final declaration but sharing many of its general principles.]

Nature has made men free and equal; the distinctions necessary to the social order can only be founded on general utility.

Every man is born with inalienable and imprescriptible rights; these are the freedom of all his opinions; the care of his honor and his life; the right of property; the entire disposition of his own person, his industry, and all his faculties; the communication of his thoughts by all possible means; the pursuit of well-being and resistance to oppression.

The exercise of natural rights has no other limits than those which assure their enjoyment to all other members of society.

No man may be subjected to laws other than those consented to by him or his representatives, previously promulgated and legally applied.

The principle of all sovereignty resides in the nation. . . .

[Five other principles followed.]

12

DUKE MATHIEU DE MONTMORENCY

August 1, 1789

When Lafayette spoke on July 11, the deputies applauded but did not follow his lead, voting to send his project for discussion in subcommittees. But when the Bastille prison fell to armed Parisians on July 14, the balance of power shifted in favor of those demanding more power for the legislature and an immediate declaration of rights. A fundamental debate took place August 1–4, 1789. The young Mathieu Jean, Duke de Montmorency (1767–1826), was closely allied to Lafayette and the reforming faction of nobles. Like Lafayette, he had fought in the American war. His speech in favor of a declaration caused a sensation.

To raise up an edifice, it is necessary to lay foundations; one does not draw conclusions without having posed principles; and before choosing for oneself the means and starting along a path, one must be assured of

---

the endpoint. It is important to declare the rights of man before the constitution, because the constitution is only the continuation, the conclusion of this declaration. This is a truth that the examples of America and of many other peoples and the speech of the archbishop of Bordeaux [a previous speaker] have made tangible

The rights of man in society are eternal; no sanction is needed to recognize them.

Some have spoken of provisionally adopting this declaration; but do they believe that we could reject it later? The rights of man are invariable like justice, eternal like reason; they apply to all times and all countries.

I would wish that the declaration be clear, simple, and precise; that it be within the reach of those who would be least able to comprehend it.

These are not detestable principles that the representatives of the nation should fear to bring into the light! We are no longer in those times of barbarism when prejudices took the place of reason. Truth leads to happiness. Would we be here if the lights of wisdom had not dissipated the darkness that covered our horizon? Would we be finally at the point where we are now?

But must a declaration of rights confine itself to this sole result? This is the first question. The second regards its form: you have been presented two of them [choices of form, essentially long or short] for the declaration; which one will you choose?

To abridge, to simplify, it would be necessary to avoid having as many declarations as there are individuals. We could take, for example, the declaration of Monsieur Abbé Sieyès [already in circulation] and discuss it article by article.

Another question, no less important, is whether the declaration of rights will be accompanied by a detailed explanation.

I have asked myself what disadvantages that might produce.

There are no doubt some truths which are in all hearts, and it is not necessary to prove to a man that he is free; will he be more free when you have proved it to him? That is only one objection. Many peoples are ignorant of this liberty, being unaware of its extent and its products. Let us follow the example of the United States: they have set a great example in the new hemisphere; let us give one to the universe, let us offer a model worthy of admiration.

13

MALOUET

August 1, 1789

Many deputies resisted the idea of a declaration of rights, arguing that the American example did not apply to a large country like France with a long feudal past of inequalities. They opposed what they considered a diversion into metaphysical discussions at a critical moment when public order threatened to disintegrate. Pierre Victor Malouet (1740–1814), a lawyer and government administrator, captured many of the reservations of these more conservative deputies.

Sirs, it is with uneasiness and regret for the time that is passing and for the disorders that are accumulating that I take the floor. The moment in which we find ourselves requires more action and reflection than speechifying. The nation is waiting for us; it wants order, peace, and protective laws. . . .

The question that occupies you still at present, and such is the disadvantage of all metaphysical discussion, it presents, I would say, an equal number of objections and of grounds for and against.

One wishes to have a declaration of the rights of man because it is useful. . . . You have been shown the advantage of publishing, of consecrating all the truths that serve as beacon, rallying point, and asylum to men scattered around the globe. To this is opposed the danger of declaring in an absolute manner the general principles of natural right, without modification by actual laws. Finally, on the side of the disadvantages and misfortunes produced by ignorance, you have seen the perils and disorders that originate in partial knowledge and in the false application of principles. . . .

I know that the Americans have not taken similar precautions; they took man from the bosom of nature and presented him to the universe in all his primitive sovereignty. But American society, newly formed, is composed in its totality of landowners already accustomed to equality, foreigners to luxury as well as to poverty, barely acquainted with the

---

Archives parlementaires, 8 (Paris, 1875): 221–22, 320, 322–23.

yoke of taxes or the prejudices that dominate us, having found on the land that they cultivate no trace of feudalism. Such men were without doubt prepared to receive liberty in all its vigor: for their tastes, their customs, their position called them to democracy.

But we, Sirs, we have for fellow citizens an immense multitude of men without property who expect above all their subsistence from an assured labor, right regulation, and continual protection; they become angry sometimes, not without just cause, at the spectacle of luxury and opulence.

It should not be believed that I conclude from this that this class of citizens does not have an equal right to liberty. Far be it from me such a thought. Liberty should be like the morning star which shines for everyone. But I believe, Sirs, that it is necessary in a large empire for men placed by circumstances in a dependent condition to see the just limits on as much as the extension of natural liberty. . . .

Since the rights of man in society should be developed and guaranteed by [a good constitution], their declaration should be the introduction to it; but this legislative declaration is necessarily remote from the metaphysical statement and abstract definitions that have been proposed. . . . Why begin therefore by transporting man to a high mountain and showing him his empire without limits, when on climbing down he must find limits at each step?

Will you tell him that he has the free disposition of his person before he has been forever dispensed from having to serve against his will in the army or the navy? That he has the free disposition of his goods before the customs and local laws that dispose of it against his will are abrogated? Will you tell him that in poverty he has the right to assistance from everyone, while he invokes perhaps in vain the pity of passers-by, while to the shame of our laws and customs no legislative precaution attaches the unfortunate to society even as misery separates them from it? It is therefore indispensable to compare the declaration of rights and to make it concordant with the necessary and obligated state in which the man for whom it was written finds himself. . . .

In [our present] circumstances, an express declaration of the general and absolute principles of natural liberty and equality can shatter necessary bonds. Only the constitution can save us from a general break up. I propose, therefore, to accelerate its drafting by taking instruction from the work of the committee [on the constitution] and by postponing for future consideration the drawing up of a declaration of rights.

The Declaration

14

"Declaration of the Rights of Man and Citizen"
August 26, 1789

Once they had agreed on the necessity of drafting a declaration of rights, the deputies of the National Assembly still faced the daunting task of composing one that a majority could accept. The debate raised several questions: Should the declaration be short and limited to general principles, or should it include a long explanation of the significance of each article? Should the declaration include a list of duties or only rights? And what precisely were "the natural, inalienable, and sacred rights of man"? After several days of debate and voting, the deputies decided to suspend their deliberations on the declaration, having agreed on seventeen articles. These laid out a new vision of government, in which protection of natural rights replaced the will of the king as the justification for authority. Many of the reforms favored by Enlightenment writers appeared in the declaration: freedom of religion, freedom of the press, no taxation without representation, elimination of excessive punishments, and various safeguards against arbitrary administration.

The representatives of the French people, constituted as a National Assembly, and considering that ignorance, neglect, or contempt of the rights of man are the sole causes of public misfortunes and governmental corruption, have resolved to set forth in a solemn declaration the natural, inalienable, and sacred rights of man: so that by being constantly present to all the members of the social body this declaration may always remind them of their rights and duties; so that by being liable at every moment to comparison with the aim of any and all political institutions the acts of the legislative and executive powers may be the more fully respected; and so that by being founded henceforward on simple and

La Constitution française, Présentée au Roi par l'Assemblée Nationale, le 3 septembre 1791 (Paris: De l'Imprimerie de Baudoin, 1791).

incontestable principles the demands of the citizens may always tend toward maintaining the constitution and the general welfare.

In consequence, the National Assembly recognizes and declares, in the presence and under the auspices of the Supreme Being, the following rights of man and the citizen:

1. Men are born and remain free and equal in rights. Social distinctions may be based only on common utility.

2. The purpose of all political association is the preservation of the natural and imprescriptible rights of man. These rights are liberty, property, security, and resistance to oppression.

3. The principle of all sovereignty rests essentially in the nation. No body and no individual may exercise authority which does not emanate expressly from the nation.

4. Liberty consists in the ability to do whatever does not harm another; hence the exercise of the natural rights of each man has no other limits than those which assure to other members of society the enjoyment of the same rights. These limits can only be determined by the law.

5. The law only has the right to prohibit those actions which are injurious to society. No hindrance should be put in the way of anything not prohibited by the law, nor may anyone be forced to do what the law does not require.

6. The law is the expression of the general will. All citizens have the right to take part, in person or by their representatives, in its formation. It must be the same for everyone whether it protects or penalizes. All citizens being equal in its eyes are equally admissible to all public dignities, offices, and employments, according to their ability, and with no other distinction than that of their virtues and talents.

7. No man may be indicted, arrested, or detained except in cases determined by the law and according to the forms which it has prescribed. Those who seek, expedite, execute, or cause to be executed arbitrary orders should be punished; but citizens summoned or seized by virtue of the law should obey instantly, and not render themselves guilty by resistance.

8. Only strictly and obviously necessary punishments may be established by the law, and no one may be punished except by virtue of a law established and promulgated before the time of the offense, and legally applied.

9. Every man being presumed innocent until judged guilty, if it is deemed indispensable to arrest him, all rigor unnecessary to securing his person should be severely repressed by the law.

10. No one should be disturbed for his opinions, even in religion, provided that their manifestation does not trouble public order as established by law.

11. The free communication of thoughts and opinions is one of the most precious of the rights of man. Every citizen may therefore speak, write, and print freely, if he accepts his own responsibility for any abuse of this liberty in the cases set by the law.

12. The safeguard of the rights of man and the citizen requires public powers. These powers are therefore instituted for the advantage of all, and not for the private benefit of those to whom they are entrusted.

13. For maintenance of public authority and for expenses of administration, common taxation is indispensable. It should be apportioned equally among all the citizens according to their capacity to pay.

14. All citizens have the right, by themselves or through their representatives, to have demonstrated to them the necessity of public taxes, to consent to them freely, to follow the use made of the proceeds, and to determine the means of apportionment, assessment, and collection, and the duration of them.

15. Society has the right to hold accountable every public agent of the administration.

16. Any society in which the guarantee of rights is not assured or the separation of powers not settled has no constitution.

17. Property being an inviolable and sacred right, no one may be deprived of it except when public necessity, certified by law, obviously requires it, and on the condition of a just compensation in advance.

3

Debates over Citizenship and Rights during the Revolution

The Poor and the Propertied

Although the status of Protestants, Jews, and free blacks would soon elicit passionate debates, the deputies agreed with little opposition to exclude servants, the propertyless, and the poor from voting and the less than prosperous from holding office.

Such views were common in the eighteenth century. Locke and most political theorists had argued that property provided an essential basis for participation in the public sphere; they generally overlooked the problem of women who owned property (especially widows and single women), putting them in the same category as the propertyless. Servants were excluded almost everywhere from political participation because they were thought to be dependent on those who employed them and therefore incapable of making independent decisions. Only the independent and autonomous (property-owning men) could participate fully in political life.

Abbé Sieyès, the vociferous opponent of aristocratic privilege, provided the rationale for the distinction between active and passive citizenship. Only active citizens enjoyed political rights; everyone else—women, children, foreigners, the poor, the propertyless, and servants—enjoyed civil but not political rights. On September 29, 1789, the National Assembly voted to divide the male citizens in three parts: the "passive" citizens who enjoyed civil rights but could not vote or hold office because they did not pay a high enough level of taxation; the "active" citizens who could vote at the lowest-level assemblies; and those among the active citizens who were eligible to actually hold office and vote in regional-level elections. Among the few who opposed this decision was Maximilien Robespierre, a deputy destined to play the role of major spokesman for the government in 1793–1794, the period known as the Terror. In contrast to most deputies, he interpreted the Declaration of the Rights of Man and Citizen as a mandate for democratic government.

15

ABBÉ SIEYÈS

Preliminary to the French Constitution

August 1789

After having set forth the *natural and civil rights* of the citizens, the plan that we are following leads us to recognize their *political* rights.

The difference between these two kinds of rights consists in the natural and civil rights being those *for* which the maintenance and development of society is constituted and the political rights being those *by* which society constitutes and maintains itself. It would be better for the clarity of language to call the first *passive* rights and the second *active* rights.

All the inhabitants of a country should enjoy the rights of a *passive* citizen: all have the right to the protection of their person, their property, their liberty, etc.; but all do not have the right to take an active part in the formation of the public authorities: all are not *active* citizens. Women, at least in the present state, children, foreigners, those who contribute nothing to maintaining the public establishment, should have no active influence on public affairs. All can enjoy the advantages of society; but those alone who contribute to the public establishment are like the true shareholders in the great social enterprise. They alone are the true active citizens, the true members of the association.

Abbé Sieyès, *Préliminaire de la constitution française* (Paris: Chez Baudoin, 1789). First published in July 1789 but expanded in August. The August version is used here.

16

THOURET

Report on the Basis of Political Eligibility

September 29, 1789

Jacques Guillaume Thouret (1746–1794), a lawyer from Rouen, spoke for the Constitutional Committee of the National Assembly that included among others Sieyès and Rabaut Saint Etienne. His report formed the basis for the subsequent legislation on qualifications for voting and officeholding.

The number of individuals in France is about 26 million; but according to calculations that seem to be very definite, the number of *active* citizens, with deductions made for women, minors, and all those who are deprived of *political rights* for legitimate reasons, is reduced to one-sixth of the total population. One must only count therefore about 4,400,000 citizens qualifying to vote in the primary assemblies of their canton [local administrative unit]. . . .

The Committee proposes that the necessary qualifications for the title of active citizen in the *primary* assembly of the canton be: 1) to be French or to have become French; 2) to have reached one's majority [be a legal adult; the age was set at 25]; 3) to have resided in the canton for at least one year; 4) to pay direct taxes at a rate equal to the local value of three days of work, a value that will be assessed in monetary terms by local officials; 5) to not be at the moment a servant, that is to say, in personal relationships that are all too incompatible with the independence necessary to the exercise of political rights.

To be eligible for office, either at the town or departmental level, one must have fulfilled all the conditions cited above with the sole difference that instead of paying a direct tax equal to the local value of three days of work, one must pay one equal to the value of ten days of work.

Archives parlementaires 9 (Paris, 1877): 203–4.

17

Speech of Robespierre Denouncing the New Conditions of Eligibility

October 22, 1789

Few deputies opposed the property requirements for voting and holding office. One of the few who did, Maximilien Robespierre (1758–1794), a lawyer from Arras in northern France, made a reputation for himself as a determined and devoted defender of "the people," that is, for the most democratic possible interpretation (still, however, excluding women) of the Declaration of the Rights of Man and Citizen and of the constitution under deliberation. In the debate about the status of Jews, for instance, Robespierre insisted on their right to citizenship. In the debate about property requirements, Robespierre invoked the Declaration of the Rights of Man and Citizen as justification for his position.

All citizens, whoever they are, have the right to aspire to all levels of officeholding. Nothing is more in line with your declaration of rights, according to which all privileges, all distinctions, all exceptions must disappear. The Constitution establishes that sovereignty resides in the people, in all the individuals of the people. Each individual therefore has the right to participate in making the law which governs him and in the administration of the public good which is his own. If not, it is not true that all men are equal in rights, that every man is a citizen. If he who only pays a tax equivalent to a day of work has fewer rights than he who pays the equivalent to three days of work, and he who pays at the level of ten days has more rights than he whose tax only equals the value of three, then he who enjoys 100,000 *livres* [French pounds] of revenue has 100 times as many rights as he who only has 1,000 *livres* of revenue. It follows from all your decrees that every citizen has the right to participate in making the law and consequently that of being an elector or eligible for office without distinction of wealth.

Archives parlementaires 9 (Paris, 1877): 479.

Religious Minorities and Questionable Professions

On December 21, 1789, a deputy raised the question of the status of non-Catholics under the new regime; his intervention started a long debate that quickly expanded to cover Jews, actors, and executioners, all of them excluded from various rights before 1789. Jews enjoyed certain rights within their own religious communities but were largely excluded from broader political and civil rights and in fact faced great restrictions on their choice of occupation, ability to own property, and the like. Actors and executioners both exercised professions that were considered "infamous"; actors took someone else's role on the stage and were reputed to be immoral in their behavior, and executioners killed people, an act considered murder under other circumstances. As a consequence, neither actors nor executioners could vote or hold local offices before 1789, and they were often shunned.

18

BRUNET DE LATUQUE

December 21, 1789

Pierre Brunet de Latuque (1757–1824), a lawyer from the Bordeaux region where many Calvinists lived, raised the question of non-Catholics in regard to the organization of new municipal and regional elections. Protestants had exercised some influence on the local level in the past, but now their opponents argued that they could not hold office in the new regime because the National Assembly had not explicitly revoked any of the monarchy's previous decrees denying Protestants the right to hold office.

Archives parlementaires 10 (Paris, 1878): 693–94.

Sirs, the epoch of the suppression of abuses has arrived; the rights of man and citizen have been pulled out from the heap of chains under which despotism had buried them. You have promulgated them; you have declared that all men are born and remain free and equal in rights. You have declared that no one can be disturbed for his religious opinions. You have decreed that all citizens, without distinction of rank or birth, would be eligible for offices and posts. You have decreed that all citizens who pay a tax equal to the value of ten days of work would be admissible to the municipal assemblies of the districts and departments [administrative units], and that those who pay a *marc d'argent* [an even higher level of taxes] would be admissible to legislative office, and you certainly have not wanted, Sirs, to have religious opinions be a reason for exclusion for some citizens and a means of admission for others.

If private interests were not constantly distorting the sovereign principles of justice, those who seek by such criminal grounds to exclude Protestants from public positions would better enter, Sirs, into the spirit and even the text of your decrees; they would take a look at the National Assembly, and seeing several Protestants sitting there in your midst, they would be ashamed of wanting to exclude from the secondary offices of the administration those whom they themselves have named to fill the offices of the supreme legislature. . . .

I have the honor of proposing to you, Sirs, a decree in the following form that requires no further interpretation:

The National Assembly decrees:

1. That *non-Catholics* who have fulfilled all the conditions laid down in preceding decrees in order to be electors and eligible for office can be elected to every level of the administration, without exception.

2. That *non-Catholics* are eligible for every civil and military post, like other citizens.

19

COUNT DE CLERMONT TONNERRE

December 23, 1789

Once the question of Protestants had been raised, other excluded groups soon came up, beginning with actors. Since Brunet de Latuque had proposed a law covering "non-Catholics," it was inevitable that someone would ask if this included the Jews, who were also non-Catholics but whom many deputies regarded as another nation altogether. Count Stanislas Marie Adélaide de Clermont Tonnerre (1757–1792), a liberal noble deputy from Paris, argued for an inclusive interpretation of the declaration of rights but rejected any separate or different legal status for Jewish communities. In his view, citizens were citizens as individuals, not as members of different social or ethnic groups. An ardent defender of the monarchy, Clermont Tonnerre was killed during the uprising of August 10, 1792.

Sirs, in the declaration that you believed you should put at the head of the French constitution you have established, consecrated, the rights of man and citizen. In the constitutional work that you have decreed relative to the organization of the municipalities, a work accepted by the King, you have fixed the conditions of eligibility that can be required of citizens. It would seem, Sirs, that there is nothing else left to do and that prejudices should be silent in the face of the language of the law; but an honorable member has explained to us that the *non-Catholics* of some provinces still experience harassment based on former laws, and seeing them excluded from the elections and public posts, another honorable member has protested against the effect of prejudice that persecutes some professions. This prejudice, these laws, force you to make your position clear. I have the honor to present you with the draft of a decree, and it is this draft that I defend here. I establish in it the principle that professions and religious creed can never become reasons for ineligibility. . . .

The professions that the adversaries of my opinion claim to mark as infamous come down to two: the executioners and the actors who occupy our various theaters. I blush to compare the children of the arts

Archives parlementaires 10 (Paris, 1878): 754–56.

with the instrument of the penal laws, but the objections force me to it. . . . What the law orders is inherently good; the law orders the death of a guilty person, the executioner only obeys the law. It is against all justice for the law to inflict upon him a legal punishment; it is against reason to tell him, do this and if you do it, you will be considered infamous.

I pass to the discussion of actors, and I will certainly have less trouble disarming a prejudice that has been weakened for a long time by the influence of the Enlightenment, the love of the arts, and reason. I will not say to you, Sirs, all that they have been and all that they can be. Several causes have motivated the opinion that attacks them: the licence of morals, and let us not forget, Sirs, that a government that never had another goal than to compel obedience often had to take measures to corrupt and that the plays, by their influence both on morals and on opinions, have been directed toward this goal by the police, one of the most corrupt branches of the former administration. . . . In any case, we should either forbid plays altogether or remove the dishonor associated with acting. Nothing infamous should endure in the eyes of the law, and nothing that the law permits is infamous.

I have said enough about the professions; I come to the subject of religion, without doubt much more important. . . . There is no middle way possible: either you admit a national religion, subject all your laws to it, arm it with temporal power, exclude from your society the men who profess another creed and then, erase the article in your declaration of rights [freedom of religion]; or you permit everyone to have his own religious opinion, and do not exclude from public office those who make use of this permission. . . .

Every creed has only one test to pass in regard to the social body: it has only one examination to which it must submit, that of its morals. It is here that the adversaries of the Jewish people attack me. This people, they say, is not sociable. They are commanded to loan at usurious rates; they cannot be joined with us either in marriage or by the bonds of social interchange; our food is forbidden to them; our tables prohibited; our armies will never have Jews serving in the defense of the fatherland. The worst of these reproaches is unjust; the others are only specious. Usury is not commanded by their laws; loans at interest are forbidden between them and permitted with foreigners. . . .

This usury so justly censured is the effect of our own laws. Men who have nothing but money can only work with money: that is the evil. Let them have land and a country and they will loan no longer: that is the remedy. As for their unsociability, it is exaggerated. Does it exist? What do you conclude from it in principle? Is there a law that obliges me to marry your daughter? Is there a law that obliges me to eat hare [like a rabbit] and to eat it with you? No doubt these religious oddities will disappear; and if they do survive the impact of philosophy and the pleasure of finally being true citizens and sociable men, they are not infractions to which the law can or should pertain.

But, they say to me, the Jews have their own judges and laws. I respond that is your fault and you should not allow it. We must refuse everything to the Jews as a nation and accord everything to Jews as individuals. We must withdraw recognition from their judges; they should only have our judges. We must refuse legal protection to the maintenance of the so-called laws of their Judaic organization; they should not be allowed to form in the state either a political body or an order. They must be citizens individually. But, some will say to me, they do not want to be citizens. Well then! If they do not want to be citizens, they should say so, and then, we should banish them. It is repugnant to have in the state an association of non-citizens, and a nation within the nation. . . . In short, Sirs, the presumed status of every man resident in a country is to be a citizen.

20

ABBÉ MAURY

December 23, 1789

Although he came from a family that had been forced to convert from Calvinism to Catholicism by the Revocation of the Edict of Nantes in 1685, Abbé Jean Siffrein Maury (1746–1817) made his reputation as a spokesman for the interests of the Catholic Church, the monarchy's authority, and the established social hierarchy. Here he attacks Clermont Tonnerre's propositions and recapitulates many of the common prejudices of the time.

The exclusion of executioners is not at all founded on prejudice. It is in the soul of every good man to shudder at the sight of him who assassinates in cold blood his fellow man. . . .

Archives parlementaires 10 (Paris, 1878): 754–56.

I go on to actors. The opinion that excludes them is not at all a prejudice; on the contrary, it honors the people who thought of it. Morals are the first law; the profession of acting essentially violates this law, because it removes a son from paternal authority. Revolutions in opinion cannot be as quick as our decrees. Some have always made use of a sophism by saying that men excluded from administrative functions are thereby dishonored; but you yourselves have excluded servants from your constitution. . . .

Let us go on to a subject more worthy of this Assembly. I observe first of all that the word *Jew* is not the name of a sect, but of a nation that has laws which it has always followed and still wishes to follow. Calling Jews citizens would be like saying that without letters of naturalization and without ceasing to be English and Danish, the English and Danish could become French. . . .

The Jews have passed through seventeen centuries without involving themselves with other nations. They have never undertaken anything other than commerce based on money; they have been the scourge of agricultural provinces; not one of them has yet known how to ennoble his hands by driving a plow. The law that they follow leaves them no time to engage in agriculture; in addition to the sabbath they have fifty-six more festivals each year than the Christians. In Poland, they have a large province. And so! The sweat of Christian slaves waters the furrows in which the opulence of the Jews germinates, and they, while their fields are thus cultivated, weigh the ducats [money] and calculate what they can remove from the currency without exposing themselves to legal penalties. . . .

In Alsace they hold 12 million mortgages on the land. In a month, they would become owners of half of this province; in ten years, they would have entirely conquered it, and it would be nothing but a Jewish colony. People feel for the Jews a hatred that cannot fail to explode as a result of this aggrandizement. For their own safety, we should table this matter.

They should not be persecuted: they are men, they are our brothers; and a curse on whomever would speak of intolerance! No one can be disturbed for his religious opinions; you have recognized this, and from that moment on you have assured Jews the most extended protection. Let them be protected therefore as individuals and not as Frenchmen for they cannot be citizens.

It should not be concluded from what I have said about the Jews that I confuse the Protestants with them. Protestants have the same religion and the same laws as us, but they do not have the same creed; however, since they already enjoy the same rights, I see no reason to deliberate on the section that concerns them in the proposed motion.

21

Letter from French Actors
December 24, 1789

Nothing is known about the actors who banded together to petition the National Assembly. They had heard of the National Assembly's discussion of their situation and hastened to claim their inclusion in the rights of citizenship. The actors adopted an almost servile tone toward the National Assembly, no doubt a sign of their long dependence on the good favor of the king and his court. Here they essentially offer their services to the new government.

Having heard that in some of the opinions pronounced in the National Assembly doubts about the legitimacy of their [the actors'] status have been raised, they beg you, My lord [president of the Assembly], to instruct them whether the Assembly has decreed something on this subject and whether it has declared their status incompatible with admission to posts and participation in the rights of citizenship. Honest men can stand up to a prejudice that the law disavows; but no one can defy a decree or even the silence of the National Assembly on their status.

The French actors, whose homage and patriotic gift you have deigned to accept, reiterate to you, My lord, and the august Assembly, the most formal wish to never employ their talents except in a manner worthy of French citizens, and they would count themselves fortunate if the legislation, reforming the abuses that might have slipped into the theater, would deign to scize upon an instrument of influence on morals and on public opinion.

Archives parlementaires 10 (Paris, 1878): 776.

22

Petition of the Jews of Paris, Alsace, and Lorraine to the National Assembly

January 28, 1790

When the Jews of Paris and the eastern provinces presented their case to the National Assembly, they leaned heavily on the precedent of granting full rights to the Protestants and on the language of human rights philosophy. They insisted that the Jews should be treated no differently from anyone else and refuted one by one all the customary prejudicial arguments used against the Jews, such as their reliance on making loans with interest (usury). Their petition shows the power of the language of rights; "all men of whatever religion . . . should all equally have the title and the rights of citizen." Despite their pleas, the National Assembly held off on granting full political rights to Jews until September 1791.

A great question is pending before the supreme tribunal of France. *Will the Jews be citizens or not?*

Already, this question has been debated in the National Assembly; and the orators, whose intentions were equally patriotic, did not agree at all on the result of their discussion. Some wanted Jews admitted to civil status. Others found this admission dangerous. A third opinion consisted of preparing the complete improvement of the lot of the Jews by gradual reforms.

In the midst of all these debates, the National Assembly believed that it ought to adjourn the question. . . . This adjournment was based on the necessity of further clarifying an important question; of seeking more positive information about what the Jews do and what they can be; of knowing more exactly what is in their favor and what is not; and finally, of preparing opinion by a thorough discussion for the decree, whatever it may be, that will definitively pronounce on their destiny.

It was also said that the adjournment was based on the necessity of knowing with assurance what were the true desires of the Jews; given,

---

Pétition des juifs établis en France, adressée à l'Assemblée Nationale, le 28 janvier 1790, sur l'ajournement du 24 décembre 1789 (n.p., n.d.), 3–11, 13–14, 34–36, 39–40, 96–97.

it was added, the disadvantages of according to this class of men rights more extensive than those they want.

But it is impossible that such a motive could have determined the decree of the National Assembly.

First, the wish of the Jews is perfectly well-known, and cannot be equivocal. They have presented it clearly in their addresses of 26 and 31 August, 1789. The Jews of Paris repeated it in a *new address* of 24 December. They ask that all the degrading distinctions that they have suffered to this day be abolished and that they be declared CITIZENS.

But moreover, how could it be supposed that the legislators, who trace all their principles to the immutable source of reason and justice, could have wanted to turn away in this matter from their accustomed manner of proceeding to seek what they should do, not in what should be, but solely in what is asked of them? . . . It is not therefore because it was believed important to know exactly what the desires of the Jews are, that the question was adjourned, but because it was judged worthy of a thorough investigation.

Their desires, moreover, as we have just said, are well known; and we will repeat them here. They ask to be CITIZENS.

And the right that they have to be declared such; the disadvantages that would result from a decree opposed to their wishes; all these grounds, and others still, will be set forth in this writing, with the energy suited to men who demand, not a favor, but an act of justice.

Finally, none of the objections made by their adversaries, or rather by the adversaries of their admission to civil status, will remain without response. . . .

If they only had to prevail upon justice, they would have little to say. But they have to combat a prejudice, and this prejudice is still so present in so many minds that they will always fear not having said enough. People argue, moreover, from their religion, their customs, their laws, as if they knew perfectly all these subjects; and it is important to draw attention to errors, which are in this regard widespread, accredited, and which perpetuate the prejudice that oppresses the Jews.

Here is, then, the plan of their memoir. They will begin by establishing the principles which require the right of citizens for the Jews. They will prove, next, that France itself would benefit from according this right to them. They will recall and combat the objections used to deny them civil status. Finally, they will demonstrate that the right of citizens should be accorded to the Jews without restriction and without delay; that is, that it would be at once unjust and dangerous to want to prepare them to receive citizenship by gradual improvements. . . .

[Then begins a detailed examination of the various charges against the Jews.] In truth, [the Jews] are of a religion that is condemned by the one that predominates in France. But the time has passed when one could say that it was only the dominant religion that could grant access to advantages, to prerogatives, to the lucrative and honorable posts in society. For a long time they confronted the Protestants with this maxim, worthy of the Inquisition, and the Protestants had no civil standing in France. Today, they have just been reestablished in the possession of this status; they are assimilated to the Catholics in everything; the intolerant maxim that we have just recalled can no longer be used against them. Why would they continue to use it as an argument against the Jews?

In general, civil rights are entirely independent from religious principles. And all men of whatever religion, whatever sect they belong to, whatever creed they practice, provided that their creed, their sect, their religion does not offend the principles of a pure and severe morality, all these men, we say, equally able to serve the fatherland, defend its interests, contribute to its splendor, should all equally have the title and the rights of citizen. . . .

[The Jews] are reproached at the same time for the vices that make them unworthy of civil status and the principles which render them at once unworthy and incompetent. A rapid glance at the bizarre as well as cruel destiny of these unfortunate individuals will perhaps remove the disfavor with which some seek to cover them and will show if it is right to make them all the reproaches that have been addressed to them.

Always persecuted since the destruction of Jerusalem, pursued at times by fanaticism and at others by superstition, by turn chased from the kingdoms that gave them an asylum and then called back to these same kingdoms, excluded from all the professions and arts and crafts, deprived even of the right to be heard as witnesses against a Christian, relegated to separate districts like another species of man with whom one fears having communication, pushed out of certain cities which have the privilege of not receiving them, obligated in others to pay for the air that they breathe as in Augsburg where they pay a *florin* an hour or in Bremen a *ducat* a day, subject in several places to shameful tolls. Here is the list of a part of the harassment still practiced today against the Jews.

And they would dare to complain of the state of degradation into which some of them can be plunged! They would dare to complain of their ignorance and their vices! Oh! Do not accuse the Jews, for that would only precipitate onto the Christians themselves all the weight of these accusations.

The vices of some of them are the work of the peoples who have given them shelter; the degradation of others is the fruit of the institutions that surround them. To say everything in one word, it is not at all the degradation and vices with which they are reproached that has attracted the harassment which overwhelms them but rather these harassments have produced their degradation and their vices. . . .

Let us now enter into more details. The Jews have been accused of the crime of usury. But first of all, all of them are not usurers; and it would be as unjust to punish them all for the offense of some as to punish all the Christians for the usury committed by some of them and the speculation of many. For a great many years now, moreover, the courts have heard fewer and fewer complaints about usury by the Jews. And, often, the Christians who accused them have given up their complaints.

Reflect, then, on the condition of the Jews. Excluded from all the professions, ineligible for all the positions, deprived even of the capacity to acquire property, not daring and not being able to sell openly the merchandise of their commerce, to what extremity are you reducing them? You do not want them to die, and yet you refuse them the means to live: you refuse them the means, and you crush them with taxes. You leave them therefore really no other resource than usury; and especially, you leave only this resource to the most numerous class of these individuals, for whose needs the legitimate interest from a modest sum of money is far from being sufficient. . . .

Everything that one would not have dared to undertake, moreover, or what one would only have dared to undertake with an infinity of precautions a long time ago, can now be done and one must dare to undertake it in this moment of universal regeneration, when all ideas and all sentiments take a new direction; and we must hasten to do so. Could one still fear the influence of a prejudice against which reason has appealed for such a long time, when all the former abuses are destroyed and all the former prejudices overturned? Will not the numerous changes effected in the political machine uproot from the people's minds most of the ideas that dominated them? Everything is changing; the lot of the Jews must change at the same time; and the people will not be more surprised by this particular change than by all those which they see around them everyday. This is therefore the moment, the true moment to make justice triumph: attach the improvement of the lot of the Jews to the revolution; amalgamate, so to speak, this partial revolution to the general revolution. Your efforts will be crowned with success, and the people will not protest, and time will consolidate your work and render it unshakable.

23

LA FARE, BISHOP OF NANCY

Opinion on the Admissibility of Jews to Full Civil and Political Rights

Spring 1790

Born into a noble family from southern France, Anne Louis Henri de La Fare (1752–1829) was elected as a deputy from the clergy of Lorraine (one of the eastern provinces with many Jews) to the Estates General. In the National Assembly, he defended the interests of the Catholic Church, and on December 23, 1789, he spoke against the emancipation of the Jews in the debate on the status of non-Catholics. He published his speech as a pamphlet in the spring of 1790, and it circulated widely at that time as part of a general discussion of the rights of Jews. La Fare repeated the standard arguments against the Jews, which held up complete Jewish emancipation until September 1791. La Fare emigrated from France in 1791 and offered his services to members of the royal family who had gone into exile. He returned to France only when Napoleon fell from power in 1814.

Thus, Sirs, assure each Jewish individual his liberty, security, and the enjoyment of his property. You owe it to this individual who has strayed into our midst; you owe him nothing more. He is a foreigner to whom, during the time of this passage and his stay, France owes hospitality, protection, and security. But it cannot and should not admit to public posts, to the administration, to the prerogatives of the family a tribe that, regarding itself everywhere as foreign, never exclusively embraces any region; a tribe whose religion, customs, and physical and moral regime essentially differ from that of all other people; a tribe finally whose eyes turn constantly toward the common fatherland that should one day reunite its dispersed members and which cannot consequently consecrate any solid attachment to the land that supports it. . . .

Opinion de M. l'Evêque de Nancy, Député de Lorraine, sur l'admissibilité des Juifs à la plénitude de l'état civil, et des droits de Citoyens actifs (Paris?, 1790).

There are only in France a small number of provinces where Jews have been permitted to establish themselves. The rest of the kingdom has but little or no relationship to the individuals of this nation. Thus, the greater part of the deputies would not know how to judge the present question with sufficient knowledge of the issue. The decision, nonetheless, is of a kind that should not be left to the enthusiasm of the emotions or to the seduction of the mind [presumably by excessively humanitarian leanings]. . . .

There are also moral and local considerations that should, if not guide, then at least enlighten the legislation regarding the Jewish nation.

The prejudices of the people against the Jews are only too well-known. From time to time, they explode into violence: recently in Alsace, some people committed the most criminal excesses against the Jews. A few months ago, similar misfortunes menaced them in Nancy [a city in Lorraine]. People wanted to pillage their houses, mistreat their persons; the animosity was extreme. Did they merit this malevolence because of criminal maneuvers, monopolies, or ventures contrary to the interests of the people? No, Sirs: the most serious reproach made to them was spreading out too much into the province, acquiring houses, lands, and privileges that the former laws did not give to them.

From this account it is easy to understand the habitual disposition of the people; it is a fire always ready to be lit. Any extension that a decree of the National Assembly would hasten to give to the civil existence of the Jews, before opinion has been prepared in advance and led by degrees to this change, could occasion great disasters. It is only prudent to foresee possible misfortunes; it is only wise to prevent them.

24

Admission of Jews to Rights of Citizenship

September 27, 1791

After several tumultuous discussions of the Jewish communities still excluded from political rights, the National Assembly finally voted to regularize the situation of all the different Jewish communities on

Archives parlementaires 31 (1888): 372. The law on the Jews was approved by Louis XVI on November 13, 1791.

September 27, 1791. Adrien Jean François Duport (1759–1798), a deputy from the nobility of Paris, proposed the motion. The deputies shouted down those who attempted to speak against it, and it quickly passed. A subsequent amendment indicated that swearing the civic oath implied a renunciation of previous Jewish privileges, that is, the right to an autonomous community ruled by its own members according to its own customs. The law required Jews to be individuals just like everyone else in France.

DUPORT: I have one very short observation to make to the Assembly, which appears to be of the highest importance and which demands all its attention. You have regulated by the Constitution, Sirs, the qualities deemed necessary to become a French citizen, and an active citizen: that sufficed, I believe, to regulate all the incidental questions that could have been raised in the Assembly relative to certain professions, to certain persons. But there is a decree of adjournment that seems to strike a blow at these general rights: I speak of the *Jews*. To decide the question that concerns them, it suffices to lift the decree of adjournment that you have rendered and which seems to suspend the question in their regard. Thus, if you had not rendered a decree of adjournment on the question of the Jews, it would not have been necessary to do anything; for, having declared by your Constitution how all peoples of the earth could become French citizens and how all French citizens could become active citizens, there would have been no difficulty on this subject.

I ask therefore that the decree of adjournment be revoked and that it be declared relative to the Jews that they will be able to become active citizens, like all the peoples of the world, by fulfilling the conditions prescribed by the Constitution. I believe that freedom of worship no longer permits any distinction to be made between the political rights of citizens on the basis of their beliefs and I believe equally that the Jews cannot be the only exceptions to the enjoyment of these rights, when pagans, Turks, Muslims, Chinese even, men of all the sects, in short, are admitted to these rights.

Decree of the National Assembly of September 27, 1791

The National Assembly, considering that the conditions necessary to be a French citizen and to become an active citizen are fixed by the Constitution, and that every man meeting the said conditions, who swears the civic oath, and engages himself to fulfill all the duties that the Constitution

imposes, has the right to all of the advantages that the Constitution
assures;

Revokes all adjournments, reservations, and exceptions inserted into
the preceding decrees relative to Jewish individuals who will swear the
civic oath which will be regarded as a renunciation of all the privileges
and exceptions introduced previously in their favor.

Free Blacks and Slaves

25

The Abolition of Negro Slavery or Means for Ameliorating Their Lot
1789

---

*The vote on the Declaration of the Rights of Man and Citizen, explic-
itly cited in this pamphlet, did not go unnoticed by those who favored
abolition of the slave trade and eventual emancipation of the slaves.
Yet even the most determined adversaries of slavery worried about the
consequences of immediate abolition, especially for the French economy.
As a result, advocates of abolition put forward a variety of proposals for
gradual emancipation and restructuring of the colonial economies. Their
proposals gained little support in the National Assembly, where the planters in the colonies had many allies.*

At a time when a new light has come to enlighten minds in all Europe;
when the French National Assembly has already destroyed the hydra
of feudalism in the kingdom; when it has established the Rights of Man
and recognized that *God has created all men free; that this liberty should
only be hampered by chains that they give themselves voluntarily, to prevent
the strongest from making an attempt on the liberty, the life or the property
of the weakest;* then slavery should only continue to exist for criminals

---

L'Esclavage des nègres aboli ou moyens d'améliorer leur sort (Paris: Chez Froullé, 1789),
3–10.

condemned according to the laws. In consequence liberty ought to be restored to that multitude of unfortunate beings, our brothers though of different color, whom European greed has kidnapped annually for nearly three centuries from the coasts of Africa and condemned to an eternal captivity, hard work, and harsh treatment.

The political interests and property rights that would be infringed if freedom was suddenly restored to the Negroes of our colonies are without doubt great obstacles to fulfilling the wishes that humanity has made in favor of these unfortunate Africans. If the French nation entirely prohibited the Negro slave trade, if it broke at the same time the chains of all those who live in our colonies, that would jolt commerce too violently; that would risk the loss of the plantations in the colonies and the immense shipping that they feed. . . . Moreover, if France alone undertook something similar, it would render itself a tributary of the other nations that possess sugar colonies and which would keep their slaves. . . .

I propose making Negro slavery like the condition of soldiers by providing an enlistment for a definite time at the end of which freedom would be restored to them. It cannot be concealed that the enlistment of a soldier is a veritable slavery, since from the moment that he contracts his engagement until its expiration, he cannot break it without being punished by death; during all this time he is neither master of his time nor of his actions; he is subject, on pain of punishment, to blindly obey the orders of his superiors; he is subjugated to fatigue, danger, to exposing himself often to an almost certain death. . . .

Being able to be kept similarly in slavery only for a limited time, the Negroes will be therefore no more slaves than a soldier: like him they will be obligated to obey during the duration of their enlistment; they will be subjugated to work of another type, it is true, but proportionate to their strength. . . .

To carry out this proposition, it would be necessary to promulgate a law that would decide: 1) That from such and such an epoch the blacks transported from Africa to our colonies could only be sold on the condition that the inhabitants who bought them would restore their freedom at the end of ten years and give at that time to each Negro a sum sufficient to pay his passage to return to his country. . . . 3) In regard to the Negroes currently enslaved in the colonies, one could divide them into ten classes for every dwelling. One would put into the first class the oldest tenth and the youngest, and the others in proportion to their age in the intermediate classes. At the end of a fixed year freedom would be restored to those of the first class and thus in the same manner as indicated above successively from year to year to those of the other classes.

By this means at the end of ten years all the current slaves will have recovered their freedom, except for those who freely took up new enlistments as previously explained. . . .

Nevertheless, if according to the representation of the inhabitants of the colonies, whom it is suitable to consult before ruling on this subject, this sacrifice on their part is judged too great, could not the state accord them a compensation proportionate to the individual value of the blacks to whom freedom would be restored? There are more than 500,000 slaves in our colonies. If the compensation was set at 500 *livres*, French money, by head, this would amount to 250 million *livres*; that is to say, 25 million a year for ten years.

26

Motion Made by Vincent Ogé the Younger to the Assembly of Colonists

1789

Vincent Ogé presented the views of his fellow mulatto property owners to a meeting of the white planter delegates who had come to Paris from Saint Domingue, the largest and wealthiest French colony. Ogé went to Paris to press mulatto claims for full civil and political rights. This document shows the complexity of the racial and hence political situation in the colonies; the mulattoes wanted to align themselves with the white planters, because they were, like them, property and slave owners. But the white planters resisted any such coalition, for they feared that such an alliance might encourage the slaves to demand changes in their status. When the slaves of Saint Domingue began their revolution in August 1791, the mulattoes and free blacks took varying and sometimes contradictory positions, some supporting the whites, some taking the side of the slaves, some trying to maintain an independent position. By then Ogé himself had died, executed for leading a mulatto rebellion in the fall of 1790.

Motion faite par M. Vincent Ogé, jeune à l'Assemblée des Colons, Habitans de S.-Domingue, à l'Hôtel de Massiac, Place des Victoires (n.p., n.d. but probably Paris, 1789).

But Sirs, this word of Freedom that one cannot pronounce without enthusiasm, this word that carries with it the idea of happiness, is this not because it seems to want to make us forget the evils that we have suffered for so many centuries? This Freedom, the greatest, the first of goods, is it made for all men? I believe so. Should it be given to all men? I believe so again. But how should it be rendered? What should be the timing and the conditions? Here is for us, Sirs, the greatest, the most important of all questions; it interests America, Africa, France, all Europe and it is principally this question that has determined me, Sirs, to ask you to hear me out.

If we do not take the most prompt and efficacious measures; if firmness, courage, and constancy do not animate all of us; if we do not quickly bring together all our intelligence, all our means, and all our efforts; if we fall asleep for an instant on the edge of the abyss, we will tremble upon awakening! We will see blood flowing, our lands invaded, the objects of our industry ravaged, our homes burnt. We will see our neighbors, our friends, our wives, our children with their throats cut and their bodies mutilated; the slave will raise the standard of revolt, and the islands [of the Caribbean] will be but a vast and baleful conflagration; commerce will be ruined, France will receive a mortal wound, and a multitude of honest citizens will be impoverished and ruined; we will lose everything.

But, Sirs, there is still time to prevent the disaster. I have perhaps presumed too much from my feeble understanding, but I have ideas that can be useful; if the assembly [of white planters] wishes to admit me, if it desires it, if it wants to authorize me to draw up and submit to it my Plan, I will do it with pleasure, even with gratitude, and perhaps I could contribute and help ward off the storm that rumbles over our heads.

27

ABBÉ GRÉGOIRE

Memoir in Favor of the People of Color or Mixed-Race of Saint Domingue

1789

Abbé Baptiste Henri Grégoire (1750–1831), a parish priest and deputy from the clergy of Lorraine, spoke in favor of minorities on many occasions during the Revolution. He had won one of the prizes of the Academy of Metz in 1788 for his essay urging relaxation of restrictions against the Jews in order to encourage their assimilation into the French nation, and he favored granting them full rights of citizenship in the debates of December 1789. He also took up the cause of the free blacks. After trying to speak on their behalf in the National Assembly and publishing this pamphlet, he continued to raise the question in 1790 and 1791. Grégoire tried to argue that giving rights to the free blacks would actually help maintain the slave system (free blacks manned the militias charged with hunting fugitive slaves in the colonies). But he also suggested that he still believed in the abolition of slavery, too.

The whites, having might on their side, have pronounced unjustly that a darkened skin excludes one from the advantages of society. Priding themselves on their complexion, they have raised a wall separating them from a class of free men that are improperly called *people of color* or *mixed-race.* They have vowed the degradation of several thousand estimable individuals, as if all were not children of a common father.…

Four questions present themselves relative to free people of color. 1) Will they be assimilated in every way to the whites? 2) Will they have representatives at the National Assembly? 3) What will be the number of representatives? 4) Do those who ask to fill this post have a legal commission? A preliminary examination of what they do in our colonies will resolve these questions by informing us what they should become.

Mémoire en faveur des gens de couleur ou sang-mêlés de St.-Domingue, et des autres Ilies françoises de l'Amérique, adressé à l'Assemblée Nationale. Par M. Grégoire, curé d'Emberménil, Député de Lorraine (Paris: Chez Bellin, 1789).

Bearing all the burdens of society more than whites, only partially sharing the advantages, being prey to contempt, often to flagrant insult, to anguish, this is the lot of the people of color, especially in St. Domingue. . . .

One rigorous consequence of what precedes is that the rejection of the people of color threatens the state with an unsettling shock; if on the contrary you fill in the gap that separates them from whites, if by bringing minds closer together you cement the mutual attachment of these two classes, their reunion will create a mass of forces that is more effective for containing the slaves, whose afflictions will no doubt be alleviated and about whose lot it will be permitted to be touched, until that opportune moment when they can be freed. . . .

The people of color being equal in everything to the whites, one will surely not ask if they should be active in legislation and send deputies to the National Assembly. Subjected to the laws and to taxation, citizens must consent to the one and the other, without which they can refuse obedience and payment. If someone could claim to possess to a higher degree this right that is equal for everyone, it would be without doubt those who, having been more afflicted by long and multiple vexations, have more complaints to lodge.

28

SOCIETY OF THE FRIENDS OF BLACKS

Address to the National Assembly in Favor of the Abolition of the Slave Trade

February 5, 1790

The Society of the Friends of Blacks rested their case for the abolition of the slave trade on the Declaration of the Rights of Man and Citizen and the granting of political rights to religious minorities. Their denunciation of the slave trade resembles in its details the account of Abbé Raynal (Document 6). The Friends of Blacks wrote in a defensive tone about

Adresse à l'Assemblée Nationale, pour l'abolition de la traite des noirs. Par la Société des Amis des Noirs de Paris (Paris: De l'Imprimerie de L. Potier de Lille, Feb. 1790), 1–4, 10–11,17,19–22.

their position because they faced intense criticism from those who feared a loss of French colonial wealth and power. They denied that they wanted to abolish slavery altogether and made a claim only for the abolition of the slave trade that transported Africans from their homelands to the French colonies. Their pamphlet insisted that opinion against the slave trade was steadily increasing in Great Britain (the British officially abolished the trade in 1807). They also raised the prospect of a slave revolt, which in fact broke out in Saint Domingue in 1791. As a consequence, many planters and their allies accused the Friends of Blacks of fomenting the revolt.

The humanity, justice, and magnanimity that have guided you in the reform of the most profoundly rooted abuses gives hope to the Society of the Friends of Blacks that you will receive with benevolence its demand in favor of that numerous portion of humankind, so cruelly oppressed for two centuries.

This Society, slandered in such cowardly and unjust fashion, only derives its mission from the humanity that induced it to defend the blacks even under the past despotism. Oh! Can there be a more respectable title in the eyes of this august Assembly which has so often avenged the rights of man in its decrees?

You have declared them, these rights; you have engraved on an immortal monument that all men are born and remain free and equal in rights; you have restored to the French people these rights that despotism had for so long despoiled; . . . you have broken the chains of feudalism that still degraded a good number of our fellow citizens; you have announced the destruction of all the stigmatizing distinctions that religious or political prejudices introduced into the great family of humankind. . . .

We are not asking you to restore to French blacks those political rights which alone, nevertheless, attest to and maintain the dignity of man; we are not even asking for their liberty. No; slander, bought no doubt with the greed of the shipowners, ascribes that scheme to us and spreads it everywhere; they want to stir up everyone against us, provoke the planters and their numerous creditors, who take alarm even at gradual emancipation. They want to alarm all the French, to whom they depict the prosperity of the colonies as inseparable from the slave trade and the perpetuity of slavery.

No, never has such an idea entered into our minds; we have said it, printed it since the beginning of our Society, and we repeat it in order to reduce to nothing this grounds of argument, blindly adopted by all the coastal cities, the grounds on which rest almost all their addresses [to the National Assembly]. The immediate emancipation of the blacks would not only be a fatal operation for the colonies; it would even be a deadly gift for the blacks, in the state of abjection and incompetence to which cupidity has reduced them. It would be to abandon to themselves and without assistance children in the cradle or mutilated and impotent beings.

It is therefore not yet time to demand that liberty; we ask only that one cease butchering thousands of blacks regularly every year in order to take hundreds of captives; we ask that one henceforth cease the prostitution, the profaning of the French name, used to authorize these thefts, these atrocious murders; we demand in a word the abolition of the slave trade. . . .

In regard to the colonists, we will demonstrate to you that if they need to recruit blacks in Africa to sustain the population of the colonies at the same level, it is because they wear out the blacks with work, whippings, and starvation; that, if they treated them with kindness and as good fathers of families, these blacks would multiply and that this population, always growing, would increase cultivation and prosperity. . . .

Have no doubt, the time when this commerce will be abolished, even in England, is not far off. It is condemned there in public opinion, even in the opinion of the ministers. . . .

If some motive might on the contrary push them [the blacks] to insurrection, might it not be the indifference of the National Assembly about their lot? Might it not be the insistence on weighing them down with chains, when one consecrates everywhere this eternal axiom: *that all men are born free and equal in rights.* So then therefore there would only be fetters and gallows for the blacks while good fortune glimmers only for the whites? Have no doubt, our happy revolution must re-electrify the blacks whom vengeance and resentment have electrified for so long, and it is not with punishments that the effect of this upheaval will be repressed. From one insurrection badly pacified will twenty others be born, of which one alone can ruin the colonists forever.

It is worthy of the first free Assembly of France to consecrate the principle of philanthropy which makes of humankind only one single family, to declare that it is horrified by this annual carnage which takes place on the coasts of Africa, that it has the intention of abolishing it one day, of mitigating the slavery that is the result, of looking for and preparing, from this moment, the means.

29

Speech of Barnave

March 8, 1790

A lawyer practicing in Grenoble before the Revolution, Antoine Pierre Barnave (1761–1793) spoke for the Colonial Committee, which aimed above all else to maintain France's hold on its very rich colonies in the Caribbean. Barnave avoided any explicit justification for slavery; he simply pointed to the need to maintain what France already enjoyed, great commercial prosperity due to commerce with the colonies. He advocated treating the colonies differently, exempting them from the Declaration of the Rights of Man and Citizen and the Constitution. The majority of deputies shouted down objections to his propositions, which were immediately adopted and included a provision outlawing anyone responsible for encouraging slave revolt.

The interest of the French nation in supporting its commerce, preserving its colonies, and favoring their prosperity by every means compatible with the interests of the metropole has appeared to us, from every angle of vision, to be an incontestable truth. . . .

Abandon the colonies, and these sources of prosperity will disappear or diminish.

Abandon the colonies, and you will import, at great price, from foreigners what they buy today from you.

Abandon the colonies at the moment when your establishments there are based on possessing them, and listlessness will replace activity, misery abundance: the mass of workers, of useful and hardworking citizens, will pass quickly from a state of ease into the most deplorable situation; finally, agriculture and our finances will soon be struck by the same disaster experienced in commerce and manufactures. . . .

You should only, you can only speak here one language, that of truth, which consists in disavowing the false extension that has been given [to some of your decrees]. You have not been able to change anything in all of what concerns the colonies, for the laws that you have decreed did not have them in mind; you have not been able to change anything

Archives parlementaires 12 (Paris, 1881): 68–73.

because public security and humanity itself would offer insurmountable obstacles to what your hearts might have inspired in you [the abolition of the slave trade or slavery itself]. Let us say it then at this moment, since doubts have been raised: you have broken no new ground. This declaration will suffice; it can leave no alarm remaining. It is only just to accompany it with an arrangement suitable for reassuring the colonies against those who, with criminal plots, would seek to bring trouble there, to excite uprisings there. These men whom some have affected to confuse with peaceful citizens occupied with seeking through reflection means for softening the destiny of the most unfortunate portion of the human race [the slaves], these men, I say, only have perverse motives and can only be considered as enemies of France and of humanity. . . .

Here then, Sirs, is the project for a decree that your committee has unanimously voted to propose to you:

The National Assembly, deliberating on the addresses and petitions from the cities of commerce and manufacturing, on the items recently arrived from Saint Domingue and Martinique, addressed to it by the Minister of the Marine, and on the representations made by the deputies from the colonies.

Declares that, considering the colonies as a part of the French empire, and desiring to enable them to enjoy the fruits of the happy regeneration that has been accomplished in the empire, it never intended to include them in the constitution that it has decreed for the kingdom or to subject them to laws which might be incompatible with their particular, local proprieties. . . .

Moreover, the National Assembly declares that it never intended to introduce innovations into any of the branches of indirect or direct commerce between France and its colonies [thus it leaves the slave trade untouched] and hereby puts the colonists and their properties under the special protection of the nation and declares criminal, toward the nation, whoever works to excite uprisings against them. Judging favorably the motives that have inspired the citizens of the said colonies, it declares that there is no reason to pursue them for any charge [there had been widespread agitation among the planters to establish greater independence from Paris]; it expects from their patriotism the maintenance of public peace and an inviolable fidelity to the nation, the law, and the king.

30

KERSAINT

Discussion of Troubles in the Colonies
March 28, 1792

As a massive slave revolt raged in Saint Domingue, the Legislative Assembly in Paris once again considered the question of free black rights (see Figure 2). Armand Guy Kersaint (1742–1793), a former noble naval officer, defended the reinstatement of the political rights of free blacks and mulattoes and argued passionately for the gradual elimination of slavery. His elaborate plan demonstrates the depth of anxiety felt by whites about emancipating the slaves immediately, but his speech also shows that the deputies knew they had to act decisively if they wanted to keep Saint Domingue at all. The white planters threatened to declare independence from France or else to ally themselves with the king against the Assembly. Kersaint hoped to establish a coalition between the poor whites and the free blacks against both the slaves and the rich white planters. After opposing the death penalty for King Louis XVI in 1793, Kersaint himself was executed in December 1793.[1]

Your fears are of three kinds: the first, the revolt of the slaves; the second, that [white planters in Saint Domingue] not call upon foreigners and not wish to make [the colony] independent; the third, that it not protest against national power [the power of the assembly] in order to only recognize royal authority. In effect, the reasons for these different fears are well-founded, but how will you succeed in dissipating them? One sole means should suffice.

There exists in Saint Domingue a numerous class of men who love France, who cherish the new laws, who are in general honest, enlightened, hardworking men who live in a state of few means from the fruits

---

[1]Information on the careers of deputies holding office in 1792–1794 comes from Auguste Kuscinski, *Dictionnaire des conventionnels* (Paris: Au siège de la Société de l'histoire de la Révolution française et à la librairie F. Rieder, 1916–1919).

Armand Guy Kersaint, *Moyens proposés à l'Assemblée Nationale pour rétablir la paix et l'ordre dans les colonies,* in *Archives parlementaires* 40 (Paris, 1893): 586, 590, 595–96.

Figure 2. Titled "Revolt of the Negroes in Saint Domingue," this engraving depicts the massive slave uprising against white planters that took place on Saint Domingue.

The Rebellion of the Slaves in Santo Domingo, 23 August 1791 (colored engraving), French School (18th century) / Musée de la Ville de Paris, Musée Carnavalet, Paris, France / Archives Charmet / Bridgeman Images.

of their daily labor and who owe no debts [poor whites]. This class is reinforced by that of the free black propertyowning men; this is the party of the National Assembly in this island; this is the class that must be supported by all means combined. [He then goes on to attack the September 24, 1791, decree rescinding the political rights of free blacks.] . . .

It cannot be denied that when the French nation proclaimed these sacred words, "Men are born and remain free and equal in rights," it did not break the chains of humankind. The action of this truth, which ought to level the world, had to first fall on us. The fears of our colonists are therefore well-founded in that they have everything to fear from the influence of our Revolution on their slaves. The rights of man overturn the system on which rests their fortunes. No one should be surprised therefore that [the colonists] have become the most ardent enemies of the rights of man; they are right to read in them their condemnation. . . .

I do not belong to the Society of the Friends of Blacks. But, as a friend of all men, I am not indifferent to the goal of the work of this society. The improvement of the lot of the Africans, transported to the European colonies, always appeared to me to be the most worthy subject for exciting the zeal of any being born sensitive to the sufferings of his fellow man. . . .

I lived for a long time in the colonies. I have owned black slaves; a part of my fortune is still in that country; and I cannot therefore wish for the destruction of it. Planters who read me, tell yourselves: He has the same interests as us and his opinions are different; let us see, let us examine; at issue here are the most cherished interests of life, and partiality and prejudice are capable of losing everything irrevocably. . . .

The moment has arrived to change the social system of the colonies, to reintegrate into it humankind, and in this greater view will be found the salvation of all the interested parties, justice and utility, interest and glory.

The free men of color demand justice: the rights of citizens in all their extension will be accorded to them. The colonists will no longer refuse them; they will remember that misfortune makes men sensitive, that those men whom they push away are their sons, their brothers, their nephews. They will honor finally the breast that nourished them, no matter what the color, and this first act of justice will guide them toward another, virtues following from each other as do vices.

Among the slaves you will call to freedom pure and simple all the artisans whose names will be furnished by their former masters, on the sole condition of a tax by head, which you will convert into an indemnity for those whom they made rich in the past.

The Negroes born in the colonies will then be called without distinction to the enjoyment of conditional liberty. It will have as its base the obligation to be reunited on the land of their former masters and to work there for them for a fixed time, after which they will enjoy liberty on the same conditions as the artisan Negroes. I think that this term can be fixed at ten years for those who are 30 years old or older, and at fifteen years for those who are less than 30 years old. But only the Negro fathers of families should be called to enjoy this advantage; the others should be held to 20 years of work. . . .

Every Negro who has come from Africa, is married for at least 10 years, has a garden in good order and six children, will enjoy first freedom for three days work a week along with his wife. After 20 years of marriage and with four children still living, they will be considered freed . . . ; their children will enjoy the same advantages at 25 years of age, and their grandchildren will be free without conditions. . . .

But some will ask if I am keeping or destroying the slave trade? My pen refuses to trace those words: "You will buy men," but this trade can change character, and the effect of the law that I propose for the colonies would modify the most odious part. It would no longer be slaves that you would export from Africa but farmers, inhabitants that you would abduct from their tyrants to educate them one day by work and instruction to the dignity of free men.

31

Decree of the National Convention of February 4, 1794, Abolishing Slavery in All the Colonies

News traveled slowly from the colonies back to France, and the first news of the emancipations in Saint Domingue aroused suspicion, if not outright hostility, in the National Convention. Many of the original members of the Society of the Friends of Blacks, such as Lafayette, Brissot, and Condorcet, had either fled the country or gone to their deaths at the guillotine as opponents of the faction now dominant in the Convention, led by Robespierre. Three delegates—a free black, a white, and a mulatto—from Saint Domingue explained the situation to the Convention on February 4, 1794. Their report provoked spontaneous enthusiasm, and the deputies promptly voted to abolish slavery in all the colonies. Their decree helped win over the rebellious slaves to the side of the French against the British and Spanish.

Décret de la Convention Nationale, du 16 jour de Pluviôse, an second de la République française, une et indivisible (Paris: De l'Imprimerie Nationale Exécutive du Louvre, Year II [1794]).

The National Convention declares the abolition of Negro slavery in all the colonies; in consequence it decrees that all men, without distinction of color, residing in the colonies, are French citizens and will enjoy all the rights assured by the constitution.

It asks the Committee of Public Safety to make a report as soon as possible on the measures that should be taken to assure the execution of the present decree.

Women

32

CONDORCET

"On the Admission of Women to the Rights of Citizenship"

July 1790

Condorcet took the question of political rights to all of its logical conclusions. He argued that if rights were indeed universal, as the doctrine of natural rights and the Declaration of the Rights of Man and Citizen both seemed to imply, then they must apply to all adults. Condorcet consequently argued in favor of granting political rights to Protestants and Jews and advocated the abolition of the slave trade and slavery itself. He went further than any other leading revolutionary spokesman, however, when he insisted that women, too, should gain political rights. His newspaper article to that effect caused a sensation and stimulated those of like mind to publish articles of their own. But the campaign was relatively shortlived and ultimately unsuccessful; the prejudice against granting political rights to women would prove the most difficult to uproot.

"Sur l'Admission des femmes au droit de cité," *Journal de la Société de 1789*, no. 5 (July 3, 1790): 1–4, 6–9, 11–12.

Habit can familiarize men with the violation of their natural rights to the point that among those who have lost them no one dreams of reclaiming them or believes that he has suffered an injustice.

Some of these violations even escaped the philosophers and legislators when with the greatest zeal they turned their attention to establishing the common rights of the individuals of the human race and to making those rights the sole foundation of political institutions. For example, have they not all violated the principle of equality of rights by quietly depriving half of mankind of the right to participate in the formation of the laws, by excluding women from the rights of citizenship? Is there a stronger proof of the power of habit even among enlightened men than seeing the principle of equality of rights invoked in favor of three or four hundred men deprived of their rights by an absurd prejudice [perhaps he is thinking of actors here] and at the same time forgetting those rights when it comes to twelve million women?

For this exclusion not to be an act of tyranny one would have to prove that the natural rights of women are not absolutely the same as those of men or show that they are not capable of exercising them. Now the rights of men follow only from the fact that they are feeling beings, capable of acquiring moral ideas and of reasoning about these ideas. Since women have the same qualities, they necessarily have equal rights. Either no individual in mankind has true rights, or all have the same ones; and whoever votes against the right of another, whatever be his religion, his color, or his sex, has from that moment abjured his own rights.

It would be difficult to prove that women are incapable of exercising the rights of citizenship. Why should beings exposed to pregnancies and to passing indispositions not be able to exercise rights that no one ever imagined taking away from people who have gout every winter or who easily catch colds? Even granting a superiority of mind in men that is not the necessary consequence of the difference in education (which is far from being proved and which ought to be if women are to be deprived of a natural right without injustice), this superiority can consist in only two points. It is said that no woman has made an important discovery in the sciences or given proof of genius in the arts, letters, etc. But certainly no one would presume to limit the rights of citizenship exclusively to men of genius. Some add that no woman has the same extent of knowledge or the same power of reasoning as certain men do; but what does this prove except that the class of very enlightened men is small? There is complete equality between women and the rest of men; if this little class of men were set aside, inferiority and superiority would be equally shared between the two sexes. Now since it would be completely absurd to limit the rights of citizenship and the eligibility for public offices to this superior class, why should women be excluded rather than those men who are inferior to a great number of women?

. . . It is said that women have never been guided by what is called reason despite much intelligence, wisdom, and a faculty for reasoning developed to the same degree as in subtle dialecticians. This observation is false: they have not conducted themselves, it is true, according to the reason of men but rather according to their own. Their interests not being the same due to the defects of the laws, the same things not having for them at all the same importance as for us, they can, without being unreasonable, determine their course of action according to other principles and work toward a different goal. It is as reasonable for a woman to occupy herself with the embellishment of her person as it was for Demosthenes [a Greek orator] to cultivate his voice and gestures.

It is said that women, though better than men in that they are gentler, more sensitive, and less subject to the vices that follow from egotism and hard hearts, do not really possess a sense of justice; that they obey their feelings rather than their consciences. This observation is truer but it proves nothing. It is not nature but rather education and social conditions that cause this difference. Neither the one nor the other has accustomed women to the idea of what is just, only to the idea of what is becoming or proper. Removed from public affairs, from everything that is decided according to the most rigorous idea of justice, or according to positive laws, they concern themselves with and act upon precisely those things which are regulated by natural propriety and by feeling. It is therefore unjust to advance as grounds for continuing to refuse women the enjoyment of their natural rights those reasons that only have some kind of reality because women do not enjoy these rights in the first place.

If one admits such arguments against women, it would also be necessary to take away the rights of citizenship from that portion of the people who, having to work without respite, can neither acquire enlightenment nor exercise its reason, and soon little by little the only men who would be permitted to be citizens would be those who had followed a course in public law.

. . . It is natural for a woman to nurse her children, to care for them in their infancy; attached to her home by these cares, weaker than a man, it is also natural that she lead a more retiring, more domestic life. Women would therefore be in the same class with men who are obliged by their station or profession to work several hours a day. This may be a reason for not preferring them in elections, but it cannot be the grounds for their legal exclusion.

. . . I demand now that these arguments be refuted by other means than pleasantries or ranting; above all that someone show me a natural difference between men and women that can legitimately found [women's] exclusion from a right. . . .

33

ETTA PALM D'AELDERS

Discourse on the Injustice of the Laws in Favor of Men, at the Expense of Women

December 30, 1790

Born Etta Lubina Derista Aelders in the Dutch Republic in 1743, she married Ferdinand Palm at age nineteen. After he disappeared in the Dutch East Indies, she eventually made her way to Paris in the early 1770s. During the early years of the French Revolution, she actively participated in the deliberations of the Cercle Social *(Social Circle), a group of reformers that included Condorcet. She gave this address at the meeting of an affiliated political club, the Confederation of the Friends of Truth, the first political club to admit women as members. In her speech, d'Aelders puts forth very general demands but stops short of making specific requests for changes in the laws. The Confederation of the Friends of Truth agitated for legislation legalizing divorce and equality of inheritance between girls and boys, and eventually set up a women's section of the club to further the rights of women. D'Aelders returned to the Dutch Republic in 1795 and took part in the revolution imported by French soldiers (her date of death is not known).*

Etta Palm d'Aelders, "Discours sur l'injustice des loix en faveur des hommes, au dépend des femmes, lu à l'Assemblée Fédérative des Amis de la Vérité, le 30 décembre 1790, par Madame Etta-Palm d'Aelders," in *Appel aux françoises sur la régénération des moeurs et la nécéssité de l'influence des femmes dans un gouvernment libre* (Paris: De l'Imprimerie du Cercle Social, 1791), 2–6.

Gentlemen, you have admitted my sex to this patriotic club The Friends of Truth [the club associated with the *Cercle Social*]; this is a first step toward justice. The august representatives of this happy nation have just applauded the intrepid courage of the Amazons [armed women who hoped to join the army] in one of your departments and have permitted them to raise a corps for the defense of the nation [see Figure 3]. This is a first shock to the prejudices in which our existence has been enveloped; it is a violent stroke against the despotism that has proved the most difficult to uproot.

Do not be just by halves, Gentlemen; . . . justice must be the first virtue of free men, and justice demands that the laws be the same for all beings, like the air and the sun. And yet everywhere, the laws favor men at the expense of women, because everywhere power is in your hands. What! Will free men, an enlightened people living in a century of enlightenment and philosophy, will they consecrate what has been the abuse of power in a century of ignorance? . . .

The prejudices with which our sex has been surrounded — supported by unjust laws which only accord us a secondary existence in society and which often force us into the humiliating necessity of winning over the cantankerous and ferocious character of a man, who, by the greed of those close to us has become our master—those prejudices have changed what was for us the sweetest and the most saintly of duties, those of wife and mother, into a painful and terrible slavery. . . .

Well! What could be more unjust! Our life, our liberty, our fortune are no longer ours; leaving childhood, turned over to a despot whom often the heart finds repulsive, the most beautiful days of our life slip away in moans and tears, while our fortune becomes prey to fraud and debauchery. . . .

Oh! Gentlemen, if you wish us to be enthusiastic about the happy constitution that gives back men their rights, then begin by being just toward us. From now on we should be your voluntary companions and not your slaves. Let us merit your attachment! Do you believe that the desire for success is less becoming to us, that a good name is less dear to us than to you? And if devotion to study, if patriotic zeal, if virtue itself, which rests so often on love of glory, is as natural to us as to you, why do we not receive the same education and the same means to acquire them?

I will not speak, Gentlemen, of those iniquitous men who pretend that nothing can exempt us from an eternal subordination. Is this not an absurdity just like those told to the French on 15 July 1789: "Leave there your just demands; you are born for slavery; nothing can exempt you from eternally obeying an arbitrary will."

Jeune Francaise allant au Champ de Mars faire l'Exercice

Figure 3. Titled "Young Frenchwoman going to the Champ de Mars to Train," this anonymous print illustrates the growing awareness of many French people that women were taking an increasingly active role in the Revolution.

Snark / Art Resource, N.Y.

114

34

OLYMPE DE GOUGES

The Declaration of the Rights of Woman

September 1791

Marie Gouze (1748–1793) was a self-educated butcher's daughter from the south of France who, under the name Olympe de Gouges, wrote pamphlets and plays on a variety of issues, including slavery, which she attacked as based on greed and blind prejudice. In this pamphlet she provides a declaration of the rights of women to parallel the one for men, thus criticizing the deputies for having forgotten women. She addressed the pamphlet to the queen, Marie Antoinette, although she also warned the queen that she must work for the Revolution or risk destroying the monarchy altogether. In her postscript she denounced the customary treatment of women as objects easily abandoned. She appended to the declaration a sample form for a marriage contract that called for communal sharing of property. De Gouges went to the guillotine in 1793, condemned as a counterrevolutionary and denounced as an "unnatural" woman.

To be decreed by the National Assembly in its last sessions or by the next legislature.

Preamble

Mothers, daughters, sisters, female representatives of the nation ask to be constituted as a national assembly. Considering that ignorance, neglect, or contempt for the rights of woman are the sole causes of public misfortunes and governmental corruption, they have resolved to set forth in a solemn declaration the natural, inalienable, and sacred rights of woman: so that by being constantly present to all the members of the social body this declaration may always remind them of their rights and duties; so that by being liable at every moment to comparison with the aim of any and all political institutions the acts of women's and men's powers may be the more fully respected; and so that by being founded

---

Olympe de Gouges, *Les Droits de la femme. A la Reine* (Paris, 1791).

henceforward on simple and incontestable principles the demands of the citizenesses may always tend toward maintaining the constitution, good morals, and the general welfare.

In consequence, the sex that is superior in beauty as in courage, needed in maternal sufferings, recognizes and declares, in the presence and under the auspices of the Supreme Being, the following rights of woman and the citizeness.

1. Woman is born free and remains equal to man in rights. Social distinctions may be based only on common utility.

2. The purpose of all political association is the preservation of the natural and imprescriptible rights of woman and man. These rights are liberty, property, security, and especially resistance to oppression.

3. The principle of all sovereignty rests essentially in the nation, which is but the reuniting of woman and man. No body and no individual may exercise authority which does not emanate expressly from the nation.

4. Liberty and justice consist in restoring all that belongs to another; hence the exercise of the natural rights of woman has no other limits than those that the perpetual tyranny of man opposes to them; these limits must be reformed according to the laws of nature and reason.

5. The laws of nature and reason prohibit all actions which are injurious to society. No hindrance should be put in the way of anything not prohibited by these wise and divine laws, nor may anyone be forced to do what they do not require.

6. The law should be the expression of the general will. All citizenesses and citizens should take part, in person or by their representatives, in its formation. It must be the same for everyone. All citizenesses and citizens, being equal in its eyes, should be equally admissible to all public dignities, offices, and employments, according to their ability, and with no other distinction than that of their virtues and talents.

7. No woman is exempted; she is indicted, arrested, and detained in the cases determined by the law. Women like men obey this rigorous law.

8. Only strictly and obviously necessary punishments should be established by the law, and no one may be punished except by

virtue of a law established and promulgated before the time of the offense, and legally applied to women.

9. Any woman being declared guilty, all rigor is exercised by the law.

10. No one should be disturbed for his fundamental opinions; woman has the right to mount the scaffold, so she should have the right equally to mount the tribune, provided that these manifestations do not trouble public order as established by law.

11. The free communication of thoughts and opinions is one of the most precious of the rights of woman, since this liberty assures the recognition of children by their fathers. Every citizeness may therefore say freely, I am the mother of your child; a barbarous prejudice [against unmarried women having children] should not force her to hide the truth, so long as responsibility is accepted for any abuse of this liberty in cases determined by the law [women are not allowed to lie about the paternity of their children].

12. The safeguard of the rights of woman and citizeness requires public powers. These powers are instituted for the advantage of all and not for the private benefit of those to whom they are entrusted.

13. For maintenance of public authority and for expenses of administration, taxation of women and men is equal; she takes part in all forced labor service, in all painful tasks; she must therefore have the same proportion in the distribution of places, employments, offices, dignities, and in industry.

14. The citizenesses and citizens have the right, by themselves or through their representatives, to have demonstrated to them the necessity of public taxes. The citizenesses can only agree to them upon admission of an equal division, not only in wealth, but also in the public administration, and to determine the means of apportionment, assessment, and collection, and the duration of the taxes.

15. The mass of women, joining with men in paying taxes, have the right to hold accountable every public agent of the administration.

16. Any society in which the guarantee of rights is not assured or the separation of powers not settled has no constitution. The constitution is null and void if the majority of individuals composing the nation has not cooperated in its drafting.

17. Property belongs to both sexes whether united or separated;
     it is for each of them an inviolable and sacred right, and no
     one may be deprived of it as a true patrimony of nature, except
     when public necessity, certified by law, obviously requires it,
     and then on condition of a just compensation in advance.

Postscript

Women, wake up; the tocsin of reason sounds throughout the universe;
recognize your rights. The powerful empire of nature is no longer surrounded by prejudice, fanaticism, superstition, and lies. The torch of
truth has dispersed all the clouds of folly and usurpation. Enslaved man
has multiplied his force and needs yours to break his chains. Having
become free, he has become unjust toward his companion. Oh women!
Women, when will you cease to be blind? What advantages have you
gathered in the revolution? A scorn more marked, a disdain more con-
spicuous. During the centuries of corruption you only reigned over the
weakness of men. Your empire is destroyed; what is left to you then?
Firm belief in the injustices of men. The reclaiming of your patrimony
founded on the wise decrees of nature; why should you fear such a beautiful enterprise? . . . Whatever the barriers set up against you, it is in
your power to overcome them; you only have to want it. Let us pass now
to the appalling account of what you have been in society; and since
national education is an issue at this moment, let us see if our wise legislators will think sanely about the education of women.

Women have done more harm than good. Constraint and dissimula-
tion have been their lot. What force has taken from them, ruse returned
to them; they have had recourse to all the resources of their charms,
and the most irreproachable man has not resisted them. Poison, the
sword, women controlled everything; they ordered up crimes as much
as virtues. For centuries, the French government, especially, depended
on the nocturnal administration of women; officials kept no secrets from
their indiscretion; ambassadorial posts, military commands, the ministry, the presidency [of a court], the papacy, the college of cardinals, in
short everything that characterizes the folly of men, profane and sacred,
has been submitted to the cupidity and ambition of this sex formerly
considered despicable and respected, and since the revolution, respectable and despised. . . .

Under the former regime, everyone was vicious, everyone guilty. . . .
A woman only had to be beautiful and amiable; when she possessed
these two advantages, she saw a hundred fortunes at her feet. . . . The
most indecent woman could make herself respectable with gold; the

commerce in women was a kind of industry amongst the highest classes, which henceforth will enjoy no more credit. If it still did, the revolution would he lost, and in the new situation we would still be corrupted. Can reason hide the fact that every other road to fortune is closed to a woman bought by a man, bought like a slave from the coasts of Africa? The difference between them is great; this is known. The slave [that is, the woman] commands her master, but if the master gives her her freedom without compensation and at an age when the slave has lost all her charms, what does this unfortunate woman become? The plaything of disdain; even the doors of charity are closed to her; she is poor and old, they say; why did she not know how to make her fortune?

Other examples even more touching can be provided to reason. A young woman without experience, seduced by the man she loves, abandons her parents to follow him; the ingrate leaves her after a few years and the older she will have grown with him, the more his inconstancy will be inhuman. If she has children, he will still abandon her. If he is rich, he will believe himself excused from sharing his fortune with his noble victims. If some engagement ties him to his duties, he will violate it while counting on support from the law. If he is married, every other obligation loses its force. What laws then remain to be passed that would eradicate vice down to its roots? That of equally dividing [family] fortunes between men and women and of public administration of their goods. It is easy to imagine that a woman born of a rich family would gain much from the equal division of property [between children]. But what about the woman born in a poor family with merit and virtues; what is her lot? Poverty and opprobrium. If she does not excel in music or painting, she cannot be admitted to any public function, even if she is fully qualified. . . .

Marriage is the tomb of confidence and love. A married woman can give bastards to her husband with impunity, and even the family fortune which does not belong to them. An unmarried woman has only a feeble right: ancient and inhuman laws refuse her the right to the name and goods of her children's father; no new laws have been made in this matter. If giving my sex an honorable and just consistency is considered to be at this time paradoxical on my part and an attempt at the impossible, I leave to future men the glory of dealing with this matter; but while waiting, we can prepare the way with national education, with the restoration of morals and with conjugal agreements.

FORM FOR A SOCIAL CONTRACT BETWEEN MAN AND WOMAN

We, _____ and _____, moved by our own will, unite for the length of our lives and for the duration of our mutual inclinations under the following conditions: We intend and wish to make our wealth communal property, while reserving the right to divide it in favor of our children and of those for whom we might have a special inclination, mutually recognizing that our goods belong directly to our children, from whatever bed they come [legitimate or not], and that all of them without distinction have the right to bear the name of the fathers and mothers who have acknowledged them, and we impose on ourselves the obligation of subscribing to the law that punishes any rejection of one's own blood [refusing to acknowledge an illegitimate child]. We likewise obligate ourselves, in the case of a separation, to divide our fortune equally and to set aside the portion the law designates for our children. In the case of a perfect union, the one who dies first will give up half his property in favor of the children; and if there are no children, the survivor will inherit by right, unless the dying person has disposed of his half of the common property in favor of someone he judges appropriate. [She then goes on to defend her contract against the inevitable objections of "hypocrites, prudes, the clergy, and all the hellish gang."]

35

PRUDHOMME

"On the Influence of the Revolution on Women"
February 12, 1791

Having made his living as a bookseller and publisher of underground pamphlets before the Revolution, Louis Marie Prudhomme (1752–1832) founded Revolutions of Paris, *one of the best-known radical newspapers of the French Revolution. In this article he responds to women's criticisms of the Revolution by attacking the role of queens and courtiers under the Old Regime and outlining a theory of women's "natural" domesticity for the new regime. Nevertheless, he calls on women to arm themselves to fight the counterrevolution, apparently seeing in the present crisis a powerful reason for quitting, at least for the moment, women's traditional*

Révolutions de Paris (February 7–12, 1791), 83:226–35. Notes are by Prudhomme, unless otherwise indicated.

peacetime roles. Disturbed by the increasing number of arrests and executions in 1793, he interrupted and then stopped publication of the paper in 1794.

Many women have complained to us about the Revolution. In numerous letters they report to us that for two years now it seems there is but one sex in France. In the primary assemblies [for voting], in the sections, in the clubs, etc. there is no longer any discussion about women, as if they no longer existed. They are accorded, as if by grace, a few benches for listening to the sessions of the National Assembly. Two or three women have appeared at the bar [spoken to the Assembly], but the audience was short, and the Assembly quickly passed on to the order of the day. Can the French people, some ask, not become free without ceasing to be gallant? Long ago, in the time of the Gauls, our good ancestors, women had a deliberative vote in the Estates of the nation; they voted just like men, and things did not go so badly. . . .

The reign of the courtesans precipitated the ruin of the nation; the empire of queens consummated it. We saw a prince [Louis XV], too quickly loved by the people, degrade his character in the arms of several women[1] [his mistresses] without modesty, and become, following the example of Nebuchadnezzar,[2] a brute who wallowed with a disgusting cynicism in the filth of the dirtiest pleasures. We saw his successor [Louis XVI] share with the public his infatuation with a young, lively, and frivolous princess [Marie Antoinette], who began by shaking off the yoke of etiquette as if practicing for one day shattering that of the laws. Soon following the lessons of her mother [Maria Theresa, empress of Austria], she profited from her ascendancy over little things to interfere in great ones and to influence the destiny of an entire people. . . .

Solemn publicists[3] have seriously proposed taking the road of conciliation; they have maintained that women enjoy the rights of citizenship like men and should have entry to all public assemblies, even to those that constitute or legislate for the nation. They have claimed that women have the right to speak as much as men.

No doubt, and this power has never been denied them. But nature, from which society should not depart except in spite of itself, has prescribed to each sex its respective functions; a household should never

---

[1] Madame du Barry among others.
[2] Nebuchadnezzar was king of Babylonia 605–562 b.c. — Ed.
[3] M. Condorcet, among others, in a number of the journal of the club of 1789.

remain deserted for a single instant. When the father of a family leaves to defend or lay claim to the rights of property, security, equality, or liberty in a public assembly, the mother of the family, focused on her domestic duties, must make order and cleanliness, ease and peace reign at home.

Women have never shown this sustained and strongly pronounced taste for civil and political independence, this ardor to which everything cedes, which inspires in men so many great deeds, so many heroic actions. This is because civil and political liberty is in a manner of speaking useless to women and in consequence must be foreign to them. Destined to pass all their lives confined under the paternal roof or in the house of their marriage; born to a perpetual dependence from the first moment of their existence until that of their decease, they have only been endowed with private virtues. The tumult of camps, the storms of public places, the agitations of the tribunals are not at all suitable for the second sex. To keep her mother company, soften the worries of a spouse, nourish and care for her children, these are the only occupations and true duties of a woman. A woman is only comfortable, is only in her place in her family or in her household. She need only know what her parents or her husband judge appropriate to teach her about everything that takes place outside her home.

Women! . . . The liberty of a people has for its basis good morals and education, and you are its guardians and first dispensers. . . . Appear in the midst of our national festivals with all the brilliance of your virtues and your charms! When the voice of the public acclaims the heroism and wisdom of a young citizen, then a mother rises and leads her young, beautiful, and modest daughter to the tribunal where crowns are distributed; the young virgin seizes one of them and goes herself to set it on the forehead of the acclaimed citizen. . . .

Citizenesses of all ages and all stations! Leave your homes all at the same time; rally from door to door and march toward city hall. . . . Armed with burning torches, present yourselves at the gates of the palace of your tyrants and demand reparation. . . . If the enemy, victorious thanks to disagreements between patriots, insists upon putting his plan of counterrevolution into action . . . you must avail yourself of every means, bravery and ruses, arms and poison; contaminate the fountains, the foodstuffs; let the atmosphere be charged with the seeds of death. . . . Once the country is purged of all these hired brigands, citizenesses! We will see you return to your dwellings to take up once again the accustomed yoke of domestic duties.

36

Discussion of Citizenship under the Proposed New Constitution

April 29, 1793

After the second revolution of August 10, 1792, a revolution directed this time explicitly against the monarchy, a new National Convention was elected to rewrite the constitution and replace the monarchy with a republic. The deputies proclaimed the republic on September 22, 1792, but drafting of a new constitution took much longer. In April 1793, the Convention took up the question of citizenship. Jean Denis Lanjuinais (1753–1827) spoke for the committee designated to consider constitutional projects. A lawyer by training and a moderate in politics (he voted against the death sentence for the king and had to go into hiding for eighteen months in 1793–1794), Lanjuinais offered the common view that women were excluded from political rights.

In laying out his case, however, Lanjuinais recognized that questions had been raised about women's place and that the original Declaration of the Rights of Man and Citizen had been vague on this point; women clearly had civil rights just like men, so why should they not enjoy political rights as well? In his report, Lanjuinais referred to the position taken by Pierre Guyomar (1757–1826), a deputy who argued forcefully, but unsuccessfully, for equal political rights for women. In other respects, Guyomar's politics resembled those of Lanjuinais; he, too, was a moderate, having voted for detention of Louis XVI rather than the death sentence.

Lanjuinais, Report of the Committee Charged with Analyzing Constitutional Projects

The general idea aroused by the word citizen is that of a member of the polity, of civil society, of the nation. In a strict sense, it signifies only those who are admitted to the exercise of political rights, to vote in the people's assemblies, those who can elect and be elected to public offices; in a word, the *members of the sovereign.* Thus children, the insane, minors,

Archives parlementaires 63 (Paris, 1903): 561–64, 591–93, 595–96.

women, and those condemned to corporal punishment or to a loss of civil rights until their rehabilitation, would not be citizens.

But in common usage, this expression is applied to all those who form the social body, that is, who are neither foreigners nor civilly dead, whether or not they have political rights; finally, to all those who enjoy the fullness of civil rights, whose person and goods are governed in all things by the general laws of the country. These are citizens in the most ordinary language. . . .

I conclude from this that the denomination of *active* citizen, invented by Sieyès, would still be useful even today; it would bring clarity to our constitutional language. . . . There are essential conditions for being an active citizen: namely, a suitable age, the use of reason, the declaration of wanting to belong to the French nation, a time of residence after that declaration which would make apparent the persevering will to belong to this nation, and not to have been deprived by court judgment of the quality of citizen or of the right to vote.

Before turning to the question of age, we must speak about sex. The committee appears to exclude women from political rights, but several projects have opposed this exclusion; our colleague Romme [another deputy] has already brought you his complaints, and Guyomar has given us an interesting dissertation on the subject.

It is true that the physique of women, their goal in life, and their position distance them from the exercise of a great number of political rights and duties. Perhaps our current customs and the vices of our education make this distancing still necessary at least for a few years. If the best and most just institutions are those most in conformity with nature, it is difficult to believe that women should be called to the exercise of political rights. It is impossible for me to think that taking everything into consideration, men and women would gain anything good from it.

Guyomar, the Partisan of Political Equality between Individuals, April 1793

I have thought hard and long about the declaration of the rights of man, whether living in France or in some other country of the world. I attached the same ideas as the Latins to the word *man*; and here is perhaps the origin of my very excusable error. In fact their *homo* expressed by itself these two words consecrated by usage, *man, woman*; I will therefore use it in the same fashion, and if I have employed the word *individual*, it is because it appeared to me more appropriate for indicating humans of each sex, of all ages, all members, in my opinion, of the great family which inhabits the world. This once posed, the first question that presents itself to the mind of a partisan of political equality between the individuals of humankind is this: does the declaration of the Rights of man apply to women? . . .

What is then the prodigious difference between man and woman? I see none in their characteristic traits. I mean soul for those who believe in it, reason and the passions for the partisans of the one or the other system. There is no doubt a difference, that of the sexes . . . but I do not conceive how a sexual difference makes for one in the equality of rights. . . . I maintain that half of the individuals of a society do not have the right to deprive the other half of the imprescriptible right of giving their opinion. Let us liberate ourselves rather from the prejudice of sex, just as we have freed ourselves from the prejudice against the color of Negroes. . . .

I think therefore that the declaration of rights is the same for men and women. I do not see what right of sovereignty could be claimed by the one which would not be immediately asserted by the other. Custom and oppression only serve to prove that power has been usurped. The law of the strongest maintains tyranny; that of justice, reason, and humanity brings us back effortlessly to equality and liberty, the bases of a democratic republic. . . .

What! At the birth of equality, would one also proclaim the enslavement of half of humankind, whose happiness we have made our project? The epoch of the new order of things will leave women in the old one, and they will date from this day their designation as islands within the Republic; they will be servants without wages, placed at the same rank that our legislators assigned to hired servants. In effect, they will have no citizenship; if they do not have the right to vote in the primary assemblies, they are not members of the sovereign. These are two empty words for them. I observe, in passing, that the name of citizeness is more than ridiculous and should be struck from our language. We should henceforth call them either *wives* or *daughters* of a citizen, never *citizenesses*. Either strike the word, or bring reality in line with it. . . .

Pressed by this argument in conformity with our principles, but pushed to a logical conclusion which could displease, I do not doubt that some will soon have recourse to the escape of a presumed representation. They will say therefore that a husband is the born representative of his wife. Following the same line of argument, charge him right away with drinking and eating for her, since surely the moral faculties are as independent as all the physical needs. . . .

Voting women incontestably have the right to be elected. . . . I do not even see any inconvenience in their admission to certain local offices, which would require no travel. The creation of free posts for women for policing themselves seems to me to be part of the system of equality established for male and female primary school teachers. This is far from the flagrant injustice that places them in a class with children, imbeciles, and madmen, all incapable of voting in the primary assemblies. This then is what men do to the women to whom they owe their perilous birth, the care of their childhood, their first education! Sexual pride makes them forget everything.

37

Discussion of Women's Political Clubs and Their Suppression

October 29–30, 1793

On October 29,1793, a group of women appeared in the National Convention to complain that women militants had tried to force them to wear the red cap of liberty as a sign of their adherence to the Revolution, but they also presented a petition demanding the suppression of the women's club behind these actions. Their appearance provided the occasion for a discussion of women's political activity more generally. Philippe Fabre d'Eglantine (1755–1794) gave a speech denouncing both the agitation about dress and the women's clubs. The Convention immediately passed a decree reaffirming liberty of dress but put off to the next day consideration of the clubs.

On October 30, 1793, Jean-Baptiste Amar (1755–1816) spoke for the Committee of Public Security and proposed a decree suppressing all women's political clubs, which passed with virtually no discussion. He outlined the government's official policy on women: Women's proper place was in the home, not in politics. Broad agreement about women's role did not prevent internal dissension among the men; Amar himself denounced Fabre a few months later and Fabre went to the guillotine in April 1794. Amar then joined the opposition to Robespierre in July 1794, which ended in Robespierre's own execution. The club at issue in the October debate was the Society of Revolutionary Republican Women, founded in May 1793 to agitate for firmer measures against the country's enemies. The

---

Archives parlementaires 78 (Paris, 1911): 20–22, 33–35, 48–51 [in both cases, I have used the rendition of the speech given in the *Moniteur universel*].

club supported the establishment of companies of amazons, armed to fight internal enemies, but it did not advance specifically feminist demands such as the demand for the right to vote. Nonetheless, the deputies found any organized women's political activity threatening and forbade it henceforth.

Fabre d'Eglantine, October 29, 1793

There have already been troubles about the cockade [the tricolor ribbon decoration used to signify support of the Revolution]; you have decreed that women should wear it. Now they ask for the red cap [of liberty]. They will not rest there; they will soon demand a belt with pistols. These demands will coincide perfectly with the maneuvres behind the mobs clamoring for bread, and you will see lines of women going to get bread as if they were marching to the trenches. It is very adroit on the part of our enemies to attack the most powerful passion of women, that of their adornment, and on this pretext, arms will be put into their hands that they do not know how to use, but which bad subjects would be able to use all too well. This is not even the only source of division that is associated with this sex. Coalitions of women are forming under the name of revolutionary, fraternal, etc. institutions. I have already clearly observed that these societies are not at all composed of mothers, daughters, and sisters of families occupied with their younger brothers or sisters, but rather of adventuresses, female knights-errant, emancipated girls, and amazons. (Applause) I ask for two very urgent things because women in red caps are in the street. I ask that you decree that no individual, under whatever pretext, and on pain of being prosecuted as a disturber of the public peace, can force any citizen to dress other than in the manner that he wishes. I ask next that the Committee of General Security make a report on women's clubs. (Applause)
Decree:
No person of either sex may constrain any citizen or citizeness to dress in a particular manner. Everyone is free to wear whatever clothing or adornment of his sex seems right to him, on pain of being considered and treated as a suspect and prosecuted as a disturber of public peace.

Amar, October 30, 1793

In the morning at the market and charnel-house [mortuary] of the Innocents, several women, so-called women Jacobins, from a club that is supposedly revolutionary, walked about wearing trousers and red caps;

they sought to force the other citizenesses to adopt the same dress. Several have testified that they were insulted by these women. A mob of some 6,000 women formed. . . .

Your committee believed it must go further in its inquiry. It has posed the following questions: 1) Is it permitted to citizens or to a particular club to force other citizens to do what the law does not command? 2) Should the gatherings of women convened in popular clubs in Paris be allowed? Do not the troubles that these clubs have already occasioned prohibit us from tolerating any longer their existence? These questions are naturally complicated, and their solution must be preceded by two more general questions: . . .

1. Should women exercise political rights and get mixed up in the affairs of government? Governing is ruling public affairs by laws whose making demands extended knowledge, an application and devotion without limit, a severe impassiveness and abnegation of self; governing is ceaselessly directing and rectifying the action of constituted authorities. Are women capable of these required attentions and qualities? We can respond in general no. . . .

2. Secondly, should women gather together in political associations? . . . No, because they will be obliged to sacrifice to them more important cares to which nature calls them. The private functions to which women are destined by nature itself follow from the general order of society. This social order results from the difference between man and woman. Each sex is called to a type of occupation that is appropriate to it. Its action is circumscribed in this circle that it cannot cross over, for nature, which has posed these limits on man, commands imperiously and accepts no other law.

Man is strong, robust, born with a great energy, audacity, and courage; thanks to his constitution, he braves perils and the inclemency of the seasons; he resists all the elements, and he is suited for the arts and difficult labors. And as he is almost exclusively destined to agriculture, commerce, navigation, voyages, war, to everything that requires force, intelligence, and ability, in the same way he alone appears suited for the profound and serious cogitations that require a great exertion of mind and long studies and that women are not given to following. . . .

In general, women are hardly capable of lofty conceptions and serious cogitations. And if, among ancient peoples, their natural timidity and modesty did not permit them to appear outside of their family, do you want in the French Republic to see them coming up to the bar, to the speaker's box, to political assemblies like men, abandoning both the diuuietion that is the source of all the virtues of this sex and the care of their family?

Decree:

The clubs and popular societies of women, under whatever denomination, are prohibited.

38

CHAUMETTE

Speech at the General Council of the City Government of Paris Denouncing Women's Political Activism

November 17, 1793

Pierre-Gaspard Chaumette (1763–1794) had seized the occasion of the Revolution to become a journalist in Paris in 1790. After August 10, 1792, he entered Paris city government. When a deputation of women appeared at city hall wearing red caps, the symbol of liberty, others present in the galleries began to cry out, "Down with the red cap of women!" Chaumette then delivered a violent diatribe against women's activism. He himself went to the guillotine on April 13, 1794, falsely condemned for organizing a prison escape.

I demand a special mention in the proceedings for the murmuring that has just broken out; it is a homage to good morals. It is shocking, it is contrary to all the laws of nature for a woman to want to make herself a man. The Council should remember that some time ago these denatured women, these *viragos* [noisy, domineering women; amazons], wandered the markets with the red cap in order to soil this sign of liberty and wanted to force all the women to give up the modest coiffure that

Moniteur universel (November 19, 1793), recounting the session of November 17, 1793.

is suited to them. . . . Since when is it permitted to renounce one's sex? Since when is it decent to see women abandon the *pious* cares of their household, the cradle of their children, to come into public places, to the galleries to hear speeches, to the bar of the senate? . . .

Remember that haughty wife of a foolish and treacherous spouse, *the Roland woman* [Marie Jeanne Roland, wife of a minister in 1792], who thought herself suited to govern the republic and who raced to her death. Remember the shameless Olympe de Gouges, who was the first to set up women's clubs, who abandoned the cares of her household to involve herself in the republic, and whose head fell under the avenging blade of the laws. Is it for women to make motions? Is it for women to put themselves at the head of our armies?

4

National Security and Limits on Rights

Rights that are guaranteed in constitutions and laws come under pressure when states feel threatened from within or without. The Declaration of Rights of Man and Citizen guaranteed freedom of religion "provided that their manifestation does not trouble public order" and "free communication of thoughts and opinions" as long as it did not lead to "abuse of this liberty." These formulations left much room for interpretation of what constituted "trouble" or "abuse." Most deputies agreed that citizens had the right to assemble in clubs but not necessarily in trade associations or unions. When nearly half the Catholic clergy refused to take a loyalty oath to the new regime, the deputies began to take action against public displays of religious affiliation (foreshadowing debates about the Muslim head scarf in the present). After France went to war against most of the other European powers, restrictions on any form of dissent grew more and more draconian. The defense of the nation in a time of war was used to justify the suppression of individual liberties.

39

Law Forbidding Workers' Guilds and Professional Corporations
June 14, 1791

The deputy Isaac Le Chapelier presented the proposed law on behalf of the Constitutional Committee of the National Assembly. Workers were organizing themselves to demand higher wages and threaten work stoppages. The deputies considered this a revival of Old Regime corporations

Archives parlementaires 27 (Paris, 1887): 210–12.

or guilds that they had officially abolished in February 1791. Most of the
deputies favored free trade in goods and labor, a position that put them at
odds with workers.

Le Chapelier: All citizens must without doubt be permitted to gather together, but citizens of certain professions cannot be allowed to gather together to pursue their supposed common interests. There are no longer any corporations [trade associations] in the state; there is only the particular interest of each individual and the general interest. No one is allowed to inspire an intermediate interest among citizens or to separate them from the public interest by invoking a corporative spirit.

Article 1

The destruction of all forms of corporation [trade association] among citizens of the same status or profession being one of the fundamental bases of the French constitution, it is forbidden to re-establish them under any pretext or in any form. . . .

Article 8

All gatherings composed of artisans, workers, journeymen, day-workers, or incited by them against the free exercise of industry and of work belonging to any kind of person and under any kind of condition mutually agreed upon or against the action of the police and the execution of judgments rendered in this matter, as well as against public auctions and adjudications of [the effects of] various businesses, will be considered as seditious gatherings. As such they will be dispersed by the agents of public order whenever legal requests are made to them to that effect, and the authors, instigators, and leaders of such gatherings and all those who commit assaults or acts of violence will be punished to the full extent of the law.

40

Law Suppressing Religious Communities and Prohibiting Religious Dress in Public

April 6, 1792

The deputies took several measures to reform the Catholic Church and gain greater control over it. In November 1789, they nationalized all church properties and in return agreed to pay salaries to church personnel. In July 1790, they rationalized the organization of the church, eliminating what they considered to be superfluous parishes. In response to resistance, they then demanded that the clergy swear an oath of loyalty in November 1790. A decree of February 1791 abolished all monastic orders (both male and female) that were not dedicated to teaching or charitable work. These decisions alienated many clergy (half refused the oath) and devout believers. On April 6, 1792, the deputies voted to suppress religious organizations of all sorts, even those composed of laypeople, and they forbade the wearing of clerical dress in public.

Article 1. All monastic and non-monastic religious organizations of men or women, ecclesiastical or lay in membership, even those devoted to service in the hospitals and the care of the sick, under whatever denomination in France, whether they comprise a single house or several, are extinguished and suppressed as of the date of the publication of the present decree. . . .

Article 9. The costumes of ecclesiastics, those of the parish clergy and those of the monastic orders of either sex, are prohibited.

Article 10. Nevertheless, ecclesiastics, as well as those who have been members of the former monastic orders, may wear the costume and vestments specific to ministers of the religion every time that they are fulfilling one of its functions but not in other places, times, or circumstances.

Archives parlementaires 41 (Paris, 1893): 235–51.

41

Law on Suspects
September 17, 1793

The deputies created a special revolutionary court in Paris in March 1793 to try those accused of counterrevolution, trying to re-establish monarchy, or threatening the security of the state, but it did not convict many defendants until later in the year. Under popular pressure for swifter action against enemies of the republic, the deputies extended the definition of suspect activities by the law of September 17, 1793.

Article 1. Immediately following the publication of the present decree, all suspect people found in the territory of the French Republic who are still at large will be arrested.

Article 2. Considered suspect are 1) those who by their conduct, their relations, their speech or their writings have shown themselves to be partisans of tyranny or federalism [a movement for greater independence from Paris] and enemies of liberty; 2) those who cannot justify in the manner prescribed by the law of last March 21 their means of existence and the completion of their civic obligations; 3) those who have been refused certificates of civic behavior; 4) public officials who have been suspended or removed from their functions by the National Convention or by its agents and not restored to them . . . ; 5) those among the former nobles, together with husbands, wives, fathers, mothers, sons or daughters, brothers or sisters, and agents of those who have emigrated who have not constantly manifested their attachment to the Revolution.

Archives parlementaires 74 (Paris, 1909): 303.

42

Law Limiting Rights of Defendants
June 10, 1794

Even though the embattled French Republic had overcome most of its internal and external enemies by June 1794, the revolutionary leadership pressed for an even wider definition of enemies and speeded up the process of judgment. Only two outcomes were allowed: acquittal or a death sentence. Those accused were denied the right of defense counsel. The number of executions in Paris reached their highest point in June and July, but the deputies then organized to overthrow the men who had pushed for the law of June 10.

Article 5.   The enemies of the people are those who seek to destroy public liberty, either by force or by cunning.

Article 6.   The following are deemed enemies of the people: those who would instigate the re-establishment of royalty, or have sought to disparage or dissolve the National Convention and the revolutionary and republican government of which it is the center; . . . those who have sought to impede the provisioning of Paris or to create scarcity within the Republic; . . . those who have sought to inspire discouragement in order to favor the enterprises of the tyrants leagued against the Republic; those who have disseminated false news in order to divide or upset the people; those who have sought to mislead opinion and prevent the instruction of the people, to deprave morals and corrupt the public conscience, to undermine the energy and the purity of revolutionary and republican principles, or to stop the progress thereof either by counter-revolutionary or insidious writings, or by any other machination; . . . finally, all who are designated in previous laws relative to the punishment of conspirators and counterrevolutionaries, and who, by whatever means or with whatever outward appearances they cover themselves, have attempted an attack on the liberty, unity, and security of the Republic, or worked to prevent its strengthening.

Archives parlementaires 91 (Paris, 1976): 483–85.

Article 7.   The penalty provided for all offenses under the jurisdiction of the revolutionary court is death. . . .

Article 16.   The law provides patriotic jurors as the defense lawyers for patriots who have been unjustly accused; it accords none at all to conspirators.

A Chronology of the French
Revolution and Human Rights
(1751–1799)

1751–
1780   Diderot and d'Alembert publish their *Encyclopedia*.

1763   Voltaire, *Treatise on Toleration*.

1770   Raynal, *Philosophical and Political History of the Settlements and Trade of the Europeans in the East and West Indies*.

1781   Condorcet, *Reflections on Negro Slavery*.

1787   Edict of Toleration for Calvinists.

1788   Founding of the Society of the Friends of Blacks.

1789   *January*   Sieyès, *What Is the Third Estate?*

   February–June   Elections to the Estates General.

   June 17   Third Estate proclaims itself the National Assembly.

   July 14   Fall of the Bastille.

   August 26   Declaration of the Rights of Man and Citizen.

1790   *July*   Condorcet, *On the Admission of Women to the Rights of Citizenship*.

1791   *May 15*   National Assembly grants political rights to all free blacks in the colonies born of free mothers and fathers.

   June 14   Law forbidding workers' guilds.

   June 20   King Louis XVI and his family attempt to flee in disguise.

   August 22   Slave uprising begins in Saint Domingue.

   September 24   Rights of free blacks rescinded.

   September 27   Rights granted to all Jews in France.

   September   Olympe de Gouges, *Declaration of the Rights of Woman*.

   October 1   Legislative Assembly begins meeting.

1792   *March 28*   Rights of free blacks reinstated.

April 6   Law prohibiting religious dress in public.

April 20   France declares war on Austria.

April 25   First use of guillotine.

August 10   "Second revolution" deposes the king.

September 21   National Convention convenes.

September 22   Republic proclaimed.

1793   *January 21*   Execution of Louis XVI.

March 10   Creation of Revolutionary Tribunal.

March 11   Civil war begins in west of France.

July 27   Robespierre becomes one of leaders of government.

August–October   Agents in Saint Domingue abolish slavery.

September 17   Law on suspects.

October 30   Women's clubs outlawed.

November 10   Festival of Reason held in Paris.

November 22   All Parisian churches closed in de-Christianization campaign.

1794   *February 4*   National Convention abolishes slavery in all French colonies.

June 10   Law limiting rights of defendants.

July 27   Fall of Robespierre, end of Terror.

1795   *August 22*   New constitution approved.

October 26   End of National Convention.

November 2   New government—the Directory—takes over.

1799   *November 9–10*   Napoleon Bonaparte comes to power in a coup d'état.

Questions for Consideration

1. In what ways do the French discussions of rights in the eighteenth century anticipate those of today? In what ways are they notably different?
2. How did the Enlightenment writings about natural law, religious tolerance, and slavery contribute to the later efforts to legislate rights? In what ways did the revolutionary decrees depart from the earlier discussions?
3. Abbé Raynal's multivolume work *Philosophical and Political History of the Settlements and Trade of the Europeans in the East and West Indies* (1770) had a great influence on contemporary opinion about colonization and slavery. Why did this long and detailed book have such an impact?
4. In his hard-hitting pamphlet *What Is the Third Estate?* (1789), Abbé Sieyès examined the basis of French society and found it defective. He argued that a just society would not accept special privileges for the nobility. How did his argument against privilege fit with the growing emphasis on equal rights?
5. In 1789 the deputies to the National Assembly debated the virtues of drawing up a declaration of rights. Do rights have to be "declared" (agreed on, enshrined in law, and published for all to read) to be effective?
6. At the beginning of the French Revolution, most of the deputies to the National Assembly believed that full, active citizenship should be restricted to men with property. How did they justify their views? What arguments could be made against their position?
7. Why did the deputies grant rights more readily to the Protestants than to the Jews? What prompted them to eventually grant citizenship rights to the Jews?
8. Women never gained full political rights during the French Revolution, although they obtained many civil rights (to divorce, to equal inheritance of family property). Why were women viewed as different from men? What did women have to say about this question? Why didn't the enfranchisement of religious minorities, poor men, and even slaves have more of an effect on the status of women?

9. In the French colony of Saint Domingue, mulattoes and free blacks comprised a group almost as large as the whites on the island. What was their view of rights? Did they identify their interests with those of the whites or those of the slaves?

10. Many whites in the colonies welcomed the coming of the French Revolution but also feared its effect on the slave population. What did the deputies in the National Assembly and later assemblies think of their situation? Did they consider the colonies to be just like France or different from it?

11. The Society of the Friends of Blacks led the abolitionist cause in France after 1788. Why did their positions on slavery and the slave trade change over time? How did they defend themselves against the charge that they were undermining France's commercial position in the world economy?

12. A nobleman, Marquis de Condorcet, took the lead in making antislavery, protoleration, and pro–women's rights arguments, and his writings figure prominently in this text's documents. What link did he make between these issues? Why would a nobleman take his positions? Can positions on rights be correlated with social, ethnic, sexual, or political identity?

13. Why were workers denied the right to form trade unions?

14. Which is more important: national security or the guarantee of individual rights? Explain.

Selected Bibliography

GENERAL

Hunt, Lynn. *Inventing Human Rights: A History.* New York: W. W. Norton, 2007. A general account of the eighteenth-century origins of human rights.
Taylor, Charles. *Sources of the Self: The Making of Modern Identity.* Cambridge, Mass.: Harvard University Press, 1989. A philosophical history of the underpinnings of the concept of human rights.
Van Kley, Dale, ed. *The French Idea of Freedom: The Old Regime and the Declaration of Rights of 1789.* Stanford, Calif.: Stanford University Press, 1994. Essays on the origins and significance of the 1789 declaration.

PROPERTY DISTINCTIONS

Sewell, William H., Jr. *A Rhetoric of Bourgeois Revolution: The Abbé Sieyès and What Is the Third Estate?* Durham, N.C.: Duke University Press, 1994. An analysis of the important ideas of Sieyès and especially their foundations in writings about political economy.

RELIGIOUS MINORITIES

Adams, Geoffrey. *The Huguenots and French Opinion, 1685–1787: The Enlightenment Debate on Toleration.* Waterloo, Ontario, Canada: Wilfrid Laurier University Press, 1991. An account of changes in opinion toward the Protestants in France with an emphasis on the rise of religious toleration in official circles.
Bien, David. *The Calas Affair: Persecution, Toleration, and Heresy in Eighteenth-Century Toulouse.* Princeton, N.J.: Princeton University Press, 1960. The best account of the notorious affair that brought Voltaire into action on the side of toleration for the Calvinists.
Schechter, Ronald. *Obstinate Hebrews: Representation of the Jews in France, 1715–1815.* Berkeley: University of California Press, 2003. A wide-ranging analysis of the role of Jews in France.

SLAVERY

Blackburn, Robin. *The Overthrow of Colonial Slavery, 1776–1848*. London: Verso, 1988. Includes excellent chapters on the abolitionist movements in America, Britain, France, and Spain.

Dubois, Laurent. *Avengers of the New World: The Story of the Haitian Revolution*. Cambridge, Mass.: Harvard University Press, 2004. One of the best among many recent works on the revolution in Saint Domingue.

Popkin, Jeremy. *Facing Racial Revolution: Eyewitness Accounts of the Haitian Insurrection*. Chicago: University of Chicago Press, 2007. A fascinating collection of firsthand accounts.

WOMEN

Levy, Darline Gay, Harriet Branson Applewhite, and Mary Durham Johnson, eds. *Women in Revolutionary Paris, 1789–1795*. Urbana: University of Illinois Press, 1979. A document collection focused on women's politics.

Scott, Joan. *Only Paradoxes to Offer: French Feminists and the Rights of Man*. Cambridge, Mass.: Harvard University Press, 1996. An analysis of the paradoxes of universalism and how they affected women.

LIMITS ON RIGHTS

Tackett, Timothy. *The Coming of the Terror in the French Revolution*. Cambridge, Mass.: Harvard University Press, 2015. An account of the many pressures on the French government, 1792–1794.

Index